COLLINS

Cycling *in* SNOWDONIA & NORTH WALES

GW00373134

HarperCollins*Publishers*

Published by Collins
An imprint of HarperCollins*Publishers*
77–85 Fulham Palace Road
London W6 8JB

www.**fire**and**water**.com
www.bartholomewmaps.com

First published 2000
Copyright © HarperCollins*Publishers* Ltd 2000
Maps © Bartholomew Ltd 2000

Collins® is a registered trade mark of
HarperCollins*Publishers* Limited

Routes compiled by David and Shirley Ackerley, Ken and Pat Brown,
Dave Hill, Des James, Graham Mills and Don Williams, members of
Chester & North Wales District Association of the CTC.
Design by Creative Matters Design Consultancy, Glasgow.
Typeset by Bob Vickers.

Photographs reproduced by kind permission of the following:
V K Guy pages 5, 8, 11, 57, 85; Bill Meadows page 53;
Photolibrary Wales/Pierino Algieri page 25, /Steve Benbow page 110,
/Janet & Colin Bord pages 17, 22, 44, /Michael Dent page 33,
/Paul Kay page 71, /Jeremy Moore pages 40, 75, /Dave Newbold page 29,
/Ray Wood page 67, /Brian Woods page 94; Wales Tourist Board page 36.

All rights reserved. No part of this publication may be reproduced,
stored in a retrieval system, or transmitted in any form or by any means,
electronic, mechanical, photocopying, recording, or otherwise,
without the prior written permission of the Publisher and copyright owner.

The landscape is changing all the time. While every care has
been taken in the preparation of this guide, the Publisher accepts
no responsibility whatsoever for any loss, damage, injury or
inconvenience sustained or caused as a result of using this guide.

Printed in Italy

ISBN 0 00 448939 X
00/1/13

CONTENTS

KEY TO ROUTES

Route		Grade	Distance km (miles)	Time to allow	Page
1	Criccieth and Llanstumdwy	moderate	17 (10.5)	2 hours	14
2	Holy Island – Holyhead and South Stack	moderate	18 (11)	2–5 hours	16
3	Bala Lake Loop	moderate	18.5 (11.5)	2–3 hours	19
4	Vale of Clwyd – Ruthin to Llangwyfan	easy	20 (12.5)	2–3 hours	21
5	Caernarfon and Glynllifon Country Park	easy	22.5 (14)	2–3 hours	24
6	Porthmadog and Blaenau Ffestiniog	moderate	24 (15)	2–4 hours	28
7	Llanfairpwhgwygyll and Brynsiencyn	easy	25.5 (16)	2 hours	32
8	Welshpool and the Long Mountain	strenuous	25.5 (16)	3–4 hours	35
9	Llanfair Caereinion and the River Vyrnwy	strenuous	34 (21)	3–4 hours	38
10	The Dyfu Valley – Machynlleth and Commins Coch	strenuous	34 (21)	3 hours	41
11	The Vale of Clwyd – St Asaph and Maen Achwyfaen	moderate	37 (23)	3–5 hours	43
12	Tywyn and Tal-y-llyn	easy	40 (25)	3 hours	47
13	Panorama Road and World's End	strenuous	43 (27)	3–4 hours	50
14	Ruthin and the Cloclaenog Forest	strenuous	53 (33)	3–6 hours	53
15	Chester, Hope Mountain and Handbridge	moderate	54.5 (34))	4–8 hours	56
16	Llansilin and Lake Vyrnwy	strenuous	59.5 (37)	5–6 hours	62
17	The Denbigh Moors – Llanfair Talhaiarn and Pentrefoelas	strenuous	61 (38)	6–8 hours	66
18	Pwllheli and the Lleyn Peninsula	strenuous	62.5 (39)	4–8 hours	70
19	Llanuwchllyn and Dolgellau	strenuous	62.5 (39)	6–7 hours	74
20	Flintshire – Mold and the Halkyns	strenuous	62 (38.5)	6–12 hours	79
21	Conwy and Betws-y-coed	strenuous	74 (46)	6–8 hours	84
22	Corwen to Bwlch-y-groes	strenuous	90 (56)	5–8 hours	90
23	Oswestry and the Devil's Chair	moderate	94 (58.5)	7–8 hours	95
24	Menai Bridge to Beddgelert	strenuous	95 (59)	5–6 hours	101
25	Snowdonia – a grande randonnée	strenuous	115.5 (72)	1–2 days	106

Distances have been rounded up or down to the nearest 0.5km (mile).

Route colour coding 

undemanding rides compiled specifically with families in mind
15–25km (10–15 miles)

middle distance rides suitable for all cyclists
25–40km (15–25 miles)

half-day rides for the more experienced and adventurous cyclist
40–60km (25–40 miles)

challenging full-day rides
over 60km (over 40 miles)

grande randonnée – a grand cycling tour
100km (60 miles)

Routes marked with this symbol are off-road or have off-road sections
(includes well-surfaced cycleways as well as rougher off-road tracks)

Capel Curig

LOCATION MAP

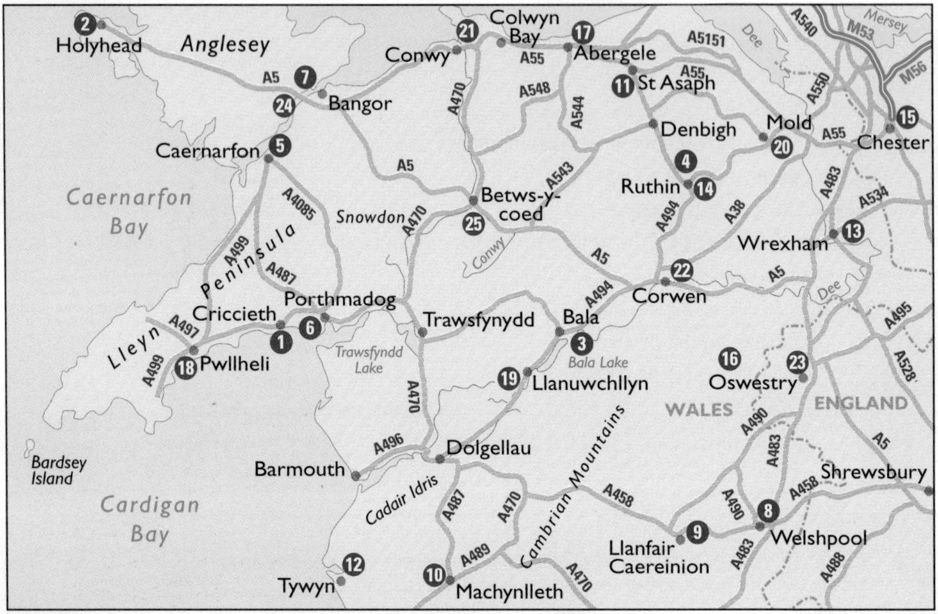

KEY TO ROUTE MAPS

M23 / Service area	Motorway		Cycle route / optional route		Telephone
A259	'A' road / Dual carriageway		Start of cycle route		Picnic site
B2130	'B' road / Dual carriageway	12	Route direction		Camping site
	Good minor road	B	Place of interest		Public toilets
	Minor road		Public house		Place of worship
	Track / bridleway		Café / refreshments		Viewpoint
	Railway / station		Restaurant		Golf course
	Canal / river / lake		Convenience store		Tumulus
	Ferry route	i	Tourist Information Centre		Urban area
50	Contour (height in metres)	P	Parking		Woodland

Height above sea level

metres	50	100	150	200	300	400	500	600	700	800	900	1000	1100	1200	1300 metres
feet	165	330	490	655	985	1315	1645	1975	2305	2635	2965	3287	3616	3945	4274 feet

INTRODUCTION

How to use this guide

Collins' *Cycling in Snowdonia & North Wales* has been devised for those who want trips out on their bicycles along quiet roads and tracks, passing interesting places and convenient refreshment stops without having to devise their own routes. Each of the 25 routes in this book has been compiled and ridden by an experienced cyclist for cyclists of all abilities.

Cycling in Snowdonia & North Wales is easy to use. Routes range from undemanding rides compiled specifically with families in mind to challenging full-day rides; the type of route is easily identified by colour coding (see page 5). At the start of each route an information box summarises: total distance (in kilometres/miles – distances have been rounded up or down throughout to the nearest 0.5km/mile and are approximate only); grade (easy, moderate or strenuous based on distance and difficulty); terrain; an average time to allow for the route; directions to the start of the route by car and, if appropriate, by train.

Each route is fully mapped and has concise, easy-to-follow directions. Comprehensive information on places of interest and convenient refreshment stops along each route are also given. Accumulated mileages within each route description give an indication of progress, while the profile diagram is a graphic representation of gradients along the route. These should be used as a guide only.

The following abbreviations are used in the route directions:

LHF	left hand fork
RHF	right hand fork
SO	straight on
SP	signpost
TJ	T junction
TL	turn left
TR	turn right
XR	crossroads

Cycling in Snowdonia & North Wales

The rides in this book run through Snowdonia and North Wales, covering an area from Conwy in the north to Machynlleth in the south, and from Anglesey and the Lleyn Peninsula in the west to Oswestry in the east, with one foray over the Welsh/English border into Chester. The routes stay away from busy main roads as much as possible to allow cyclists to discover the quiet roads and lanes, tracks and cycleways that cross this area, passing all manner of castles, historic houses, museums and other attractions, set in beautiful scenery. Much of the area is hilly, and there are steep sections to be tackled in some of the routes. However, this is compensated for by spectacular views – and you can always get off and push your bike!

Various off-road routes are followed, including sections of the Lôn Las Cymru and the Shropshire Union Canal towpath. Be aware that these routes are often designated as multi-use, for walkers and horse riders as well as cyclists.

The Lôn Las Cymru, the Welsh National Cycle Network, runs from Holyhead to Cardiff and Chepstow. It is being developed by the charity Sustrans and the network will run through towns and cities and link urban areas with the countryside. For information contact Sustrans at 35 King Street, Bristol, BS1 4DZ, telephone (0117) 926 8893, www.sustrans.org.uk. Tourist Information Centres can provide information on local cycleways. Note that you will need a permit from British Waterways in order to cycle along canal towpaths (free for the Shropshire Union Canal). Telephone British Waterways on (01923) 201120 for further details.

Geology, geography and history

North Wales is a land of mountains and lakes, forests and moorland, rivers and waterfalls, and has an impressive coastline, with high cliffs and sandy beaches. Encompassed in this area is Snowdonia National Park, covering an area of 1352km (845 miles), with the highest point, Snowdon itself, 1085m (3560 feet) above sea level.

You will see evidence of man's early occupation in the ancient stone circles and standing stones passed on some routes. The Romans colonised the area and you can still see evidence of their rule, particularly in Chester. On their departure Irish settlers tried to establish themselves on Anglesey and the Llyn Peninsula until the 5th-century Briton, Cunedda, successfully founded a strong dynasty encompassing north and west Wales. Although the Saxons conquered what is now England, they were stopped in Wales by Arthur, whose victories in the 6th century laid the basis for an enduring Welsh nation and culture. The power struggle between the Welsh rulers

Caernarfon Castle

and the English kings continued until the 15th century, when a Welshman, Henry Tudor, won the Battle of Bosworth in 1485. From this time, Welsh and English history merged and the Principality of Wales was ruled from Westminster, until 1999 and the creation of an independent Welsh Assembly. Welsh national consciousness is symbolised by the Welsh language, one of Europe's oldest living languages and a link with the 6th-century Britons. It is similar to the Breton spoken in Brittany, where many Britons settled to escape the Saxon invasion. Expect to hear Welsh spoken and see it written, particularly on road signs.

Preparing for a cycling trip

Basic maintenance

A cycle ride is an immense pleasure, particularly on a warm sunny day. Nothing is better than coasting along a country lane gazing over the countryside. Unfortunately, not every cycling day is as perfect as this, and it is important to make sure that your bike is in good order and that you are taking the necessary clothing and supplies with you.

Before you go out on your bicycle check that everything is in order. Pump the tyres up if needed, and check that the brakes are working properly and that nothing is loose – the brakes are the only means of stopping quickly and safely. If there is a problem and you are not sure that you can fix it, take the bike to a cycle repair shop – they can often deal with small repairs very quickly.

When you go out cycling it is important to take either a puncture repair kit or a spare inner tube – it is often quicker to replace the inner tube in the event of a puncture, though it may be a good idea to practise first. You also need a pump, and with a slow puncture the pump may be enough to get you home. To remove the tyre you need a set of tyre levers. Other basic tools are an Allen key and a spanner. Some wheels on modern bikes can be removed by quick release levers built into the bike. Take a lock for your bike and if you have to leave it at any time, leave it in public view and locked through the frame and front wheel to something secure.

What to wear and take with you

It is not necessary to buy specialised cycling clothes. If it is not warm enough to wear shorts wear trousers which are easy to move in but fairly close to the leg below the knee – leggings are ideal – as this stops the trousers catching the chain. If you haven't got narrow-legged trousers, bicycle clips will hold them in. Jeans are not a good idea as they are rather tight and difficult to cycle in, and if they get wet they take a long time to dry. If your shorts or trousers are thin you might get a bit sore from being too long on the saddle. This problem can be reduced by using a gel saddle, and by wearing thicker, or extra, pants. Once you are a committed cyclist you can buy cycling shorts; or undershorts which have a protective pad built in and which can be worn under anything. It is a good idea to wear several thin layers of clothes so that you can add or remove layers as necessary. A zip-fronted top gives easy temperature control. Make sure you have something warm and something waterproof.

If you wear shoes with a firm, flat sole you will be able to exert pressure on the pedals easily, and will have less work to do to make the bicycle move. Gloves not only keep your hands warm but protect them in the event that you come off, and cycling mittens which cushion your hands are not expensive. A helmet is not a legal requirement, but it will protect your head if you fall.

In general it is a good idea to wear bright clothing so that you can be easily seen by motorists, and this is particularly important when it is overcast or getting dark. If you might be out in the dark or twilight fit your bicycle with lights – by law your bicycle must have a reflector. You can also buy reflective bands for your ankles, or to wear over your shoulder and back, and these help motorists to see you.

You may be surprised how quickly you use up energy when cycling, and it is important to eat a carbohydrate meal before you set out. When planning a long ride, eat well the night before. You should eat small amounts of food regularly while you are cycling, or you may find that your energy suddenly disappears, particularly if there are hills or if the weather is cold. It is important to always carry something to eat with you – chocolate, bananas, biscuits – so that if you do start fading away you can restore yourself quickly. In warm weather you will sweat and use up fluid, and you always need to carry something to drink – water will do! Many bicycles have a fitment in which to put a water bottle, and if you don't have one a cycle shop should be able to fit one.

It is also a good idea to carry a small first aid kit. This should include elastoplasts or bandages, sunburn cream, and an anti-histamine in case you are stung by a passing insect.

It is a good idea to have a pannier to carry all these items. Some fit on the handlebars, some to the back of the seat and some onto a back rack. For a day's ride you probably won't need a lot of carrying capacity, but it is better to carry items in a pannier rather than in a rucksack on your back. Pack items that you are carrying carefully – loose items can be dangerous.

Getting to the start of the ride

If you are lucky you will be able to cycle to the start of the ride, but often transport is necessary. If you travel there by train, some sprinter services carry two bicycles without prior booking. Other services carry bicycles free in off-peak periods, but check the details with your local station. Alternatively, you could use your car – it may be possible to get a bike in the back of a hatchback if you take out the front wheel. There are inexpensive, easily fitted car racks which carry bicycles safely. Your local cycle store will be able to supply one to suit you.

Cycling on-road

Cycling on back roads is a delight with quiet lanes, interesting villages, good views and a smooth easy surface to coast along on. The cycle rides in this book are mainly on quiet roads but you sometimes cross busy roads or have stretches on B roads, and whatever sort of road you are on it is essential to ride safely. Always be aware of the possibility or existence of other traffic. Glance behind regularly, signal before you turn or change lane, and keep to the left. If there are motorists around, make sure that they have seen you before you cross their path. Cycling can be dangerous if you are competing for space with motor vehicles, many of which seem to have difficulty in seeing cyclists. When drivers are coming out of side roads, catch their eye before you ride in front of them.

You will find that many roads have potholes and uneven edges. They are much more difficult to spot when you are in a group because of the restricted view ahead, and therefore warnings need to be given. It is a good idea to cycle about a metre out into the road, conditions permitting,

Near Beddgelert

so that you avoid the worst of the uneven surfaces and to give you room to move in to the left if you are closely overtaken by a motor vehicle.

Other things to be careful of are slippery roads, particularly where there is mud or fallen leaves. Sudden rain after a period of dry weather often makes the roads extremely slippery. Dogs, too, are a hazard because they often move unpredictably, and sometimes like to chase cyclists. If you are not happy, stop or go slowly until the problem has passed.

Pedalling

Many modern bikes have 18 or 21 gears with three rings at the front and six or seven on the back wheel, and for much of the time you will find that the middle gear at the front with the range of gears at the back will be fine. Use your gears to find one that is easy to pedal along in so that your feet move round easily and you do not put too much pressure on your knees. If you are new to the bike and the gears it is a good idea to practise changing the gears on a stretch of flat, quiet road so that when you need to change gears quickly you will be ready to do so.

Cycling in a group

When cycling in a group it is essential to do so in a disciplined manner for your own, and others', safety. Do not ride too close to the bicycle in front of you – keep about a bicycle's length between you so that you will have space to brake or stop. Always keep both hands on the handlebars, except when signalling, etc. It is alright to cycle two abreast on quiet roads, but if it is necessary to change from cycling two abreast to single file this is usually done by the outside rider falling in behind the nearside rider; always cycle in single file where there are double white lines, on busy roads, or on narrow and winding roads where you have a restricted view of the road ahead. Overtake on the right (outside) only; do not overtake on the inside.

It is important to pass information to other members of the group, for example:

car up – a vehicle is coming up behind the group and will be overtaking;

car down – a vehicle is coming towards the group;

single up – get into single file;

stopping – stopping, or

slowing/easy – slowing due to junction, etc., ahead;

on the left – there is an obstacle on the left, e.g. pedestrian, parked car;

pothole – pothole (and point towards it).

Accidents

In case of an accident, stay calm and, if needed, ring the emergency services on 999. It is a good idea to carry a basic first aid kit and perhaps also one of the commercial foil wraps to put around anyone who has an accident to keep them warm. If someone comes off their bicycle move them and the bike off the road if it is safe to do so. Get someone in the party to warn approaching traffic to slow down, and if necessary ring for an ambulance.

Cycling off-road

All the routes in this book take you along legal rights of way – bridleways, byways open to all traffic and roads used as public paths – it is illegal to cycle along footpaths. Generally the off-road sections of the routes will be easy if the weather and ground are dry. If the weather has been wet and the ground is muddy, it is not a good idea to cycle along bridleways unless you do not mind getting dirty and unless you have a mountain bike which will not get blocked up with mud. In dry weather any bicycle will be able to cover the bridleway sections, but you may need to dismount if the path is very uneven.

Off-road cycling is different to cycling on the road. The average speed is lower, you will use more energy, your riding style will be different and there is a different set of rules to obey – the off-road code:

1 Give way to horse riders and pedestrians, and use a bell or call out to warn someone of your presence.
2 Take your rubbish with you.
3 Do not light fires.
4 Close gates behind you.
5 Do not interfere with wildlife, plants or trees.
6 Use only tracks where you have a right of way, or where the landowner has given you permission to ride.
7 Avoid back wheel skids, which can start erosion gulleys and ruin the bridleway.

Some of the off-road rides take you some miles from shelter and civilisation – take waterproofs, plenty of food and drink and basic tools – especially spare inner tubes and tyre repair equipment. Tell someone where you are going and approximately when you are due back. You are more likely to tumble off your bike riding off-road, so you should consider wearing a helmet and mittens with padded palms.

Local Tourist Information Centres

Bala
Pensarn Road, Bala
Telephone (01678) 521021

Betwys-y-Coed
Royal Oak Stables, Betwys-y-Coed
Telephone (01690) 710426

Blaenau Ffestiniog
High Street, Blaenau Ffestiniog
Telephone (01766) 830360

Caernarfon
Castle Street, Caernarfon
Telephone (01286) 672232

Chester
Town Hall, Chester
Telephone (01244) 402111

Conwy
Conwy Castle, Conwy
Telephone (01492) 592248

Dolgellau
Eldon Square, Dolgellau
Telephone (01341) 422888

Holyhead
Stena Line Terminal 1, Holyhead
Telephone (01407) 762622

Lake Vyrnwy
Craft Workshops, Vyrnwy
Telephone (01691) 870346

Llanberis
41a High Street, Llanberis
Telephone (01286) 870765

Llanfairpwll
Station Site, Llanfairpwll
Telephone (01248) 713177

Llangollen
Castle Street, Llangollen
(01978) 860828

Machynlleth
Canolfan Owain Glyndwr, Machynlleth
Telephone (01654) 702401

Mold
Earl Road, Mold
(01352) 759331

Oswestry
2 Church Terrace, Oswestry
Telephone (01691) 662753

Porthmadog
High Street, Porthmadog
Telephone (01766) 512981

Prestatyn
High Street, Prestatyn
Telephone (01745) 889092

Pwllheli
Station Square, Pwllheli
Telephone (01758) 613000

Ruthin
Park Road, Ruthin
Telephone (01824) 703992

Tywyn
High Street, Tywyn
Telephone (01654) 710070

Welshpool
Church Street, Welshpool
Telephone (01938) 552043

Wrexham
Lambpit Street, Wrexham
Telephone (01978) 292015

Local cycle hire

(See also Local cycle shops below.)

Bala Adventure and Watersports
Bala
Telephone (01678) 52059

Caernarfon Cycle Hire
Caernarfon
Telephone (01248) 671691

Tyn y Cornel Hotel
Tywyn
Telephone (01654) 782282

Local cycle shops

Beics Beddgelert
Beddgelert
Telephone (01766) 890434

Beics Betws
Betws-y-Coed
Telephone (01690) 710766

Beics Coed y Brenin
Dolgellau
Telephone (01341) 440666

Beics Eryri
Caernarfon
Telephone (01286) 676637

Dragon Bikes and Kites
Dolgellau
Telephone (01341) 423008

Greenstiles
Machynlleth
Telephone (01654) 703543

R H Roberts
Bala
Telephone (01678) 520252

West End Cycles
Colwyn Bay
Telephone (01492) 530269

Route 1

CRICCIETH AND LLANYSTUMDWY

Route information

Distance 17km (10.5 miles)

Grade Moderate

Terrain Generally level, quiet roads. There are a few hills for which low gears would be useful.

Time to allow 2 hours.

Getting there by car Criccieth is on the A497, off the A487. There is car parking in the town.

Getting there by train Criccieth Station is on the Shrewsbury to Pwllheli line. For travel information, telephone 0345 484950.

This route follows quiet country lanes through wooded countryside for a short circuit from Criccieth, taking in Talhenbont Hall and Llanystumdwy. There are good views of Snowdonia and the Lleyn Peninsula, and an abundance of wildlife to be seen along the way.

Places of interest along the route

A Criccieth

Overlooking Tremadoc Bay, Criccieth is a popular family holiday resort. **Criccieth Castle** was originally built by the Welsh prince Llywelyn the Great, probably between 1230 and 1240. Edward I captured the castle in 1283 and subsequently rebuilt it. In 1404 the castle was recaptured and burnt by the Welsh leader Owain Glyn Dwr. Cadw (Welsh Historic Monuments) property. Open April to September, 1000–1800. Charge. Telephone (01766) 522227.

B Talhenbont Hall, near Criccieth

Built in 1607, the hall has many attractions for today's visitor, including the River Dwyfach and its resident otters, the Quackery, home to many ducks, and a children's adventure playground. Tearoom. Open Easter and June to September, daily 1000–1700; at all other times Thursday–Sunday 1000–1700. Charge. Telephone (01766) 810247.

C Llanystumdwy

The village was home for 55 years to David Lloyd George, MP for Caernarfon and Prime Minister. A museum in the village celebrates his life. His tomb is by the River Dwy, just outside Llanystumdwy. Telephone the Tourist Information Centre in Pwllheli for more details on (01758) 613000.

Route description

Start from the level crossing in Criccieth. SO at XR, SP Caernarfon.

1 Continue uphill and follow B4411 through Rhoslan. ***5km (3 miles)***

2 TL at junction, SP Ynys/Llangybi/Llanarmon.

3 TL at TJ, SP Llanystumdwy/Chwilog/Y Ffor.

4 TL at junction beside telephone box, SP Llanystumdwy/NCN 8 (10km/6 miles). Pass Talhenbont Hall and descend steep hill WITH CARE.

5 TL over bridge and climb.

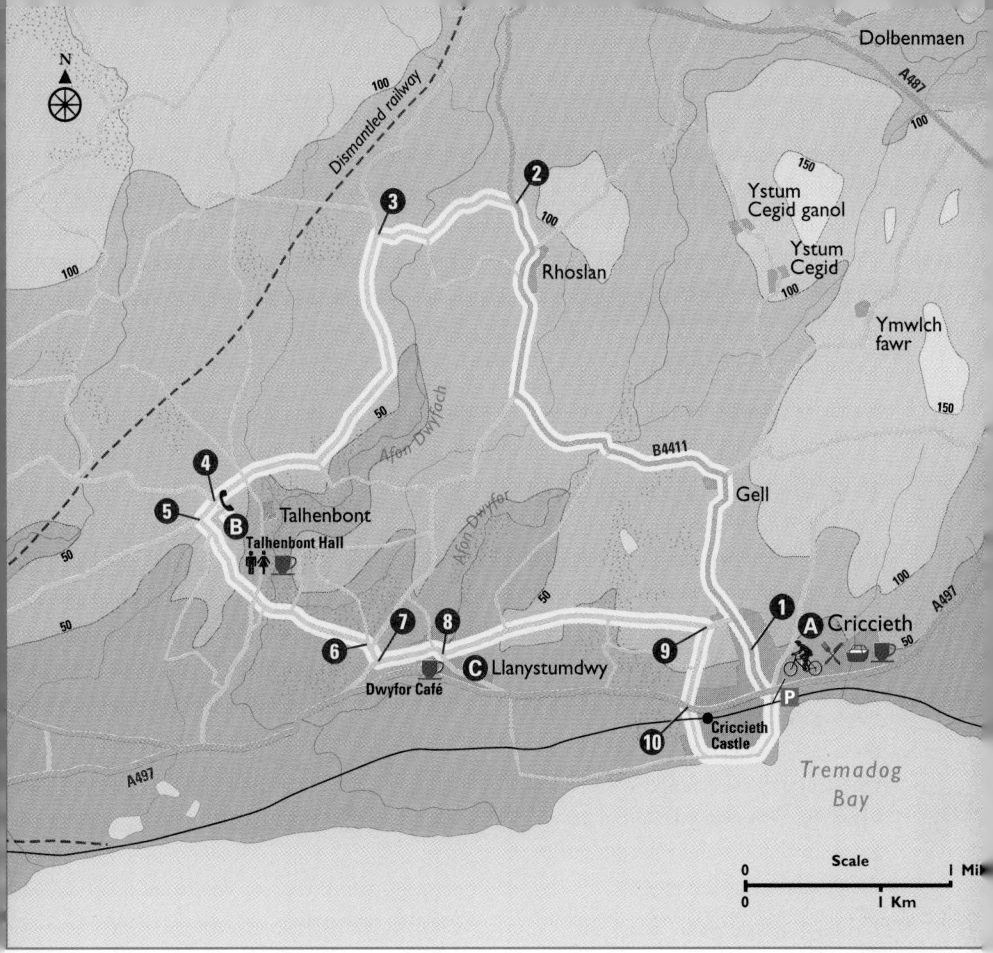

6 TR at TJ, SP Llanystumdwy/NCN 8.

7 TL at TJ, SP Llanystumdwy/Lloyd George Museum. Continue through Llanystumdwy, over bridge and immediately:

8 TL at junction, SP NCN 8. Pass Lloyd George Memorial and rear entrance to museum. Continue along this road.

9 TR onto single track road, SP NCN 8.

14.5km (9 miles)

10 SO WITH CARE at XR across A497, SP Beach/Castle. Continue past castle and lifeboat house and complete the route.

17km (10.5 miles)

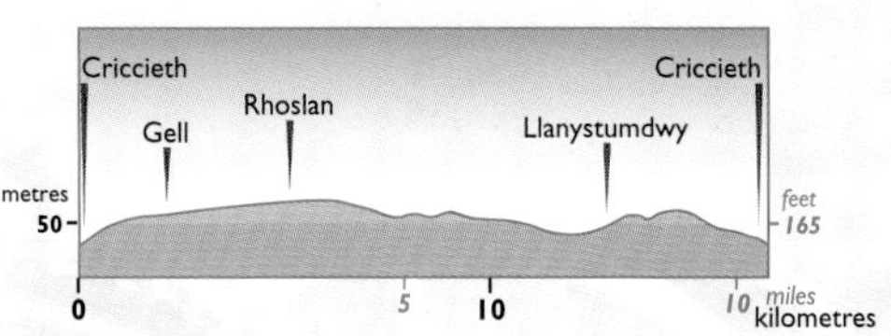

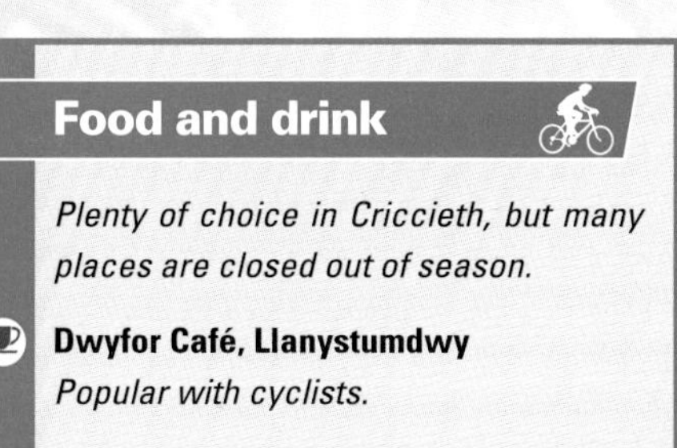

Food and drink

Plenty of choice in Criccieth, but many places are closed out of season.

Dwyfor Café, Llanystumdwy
Popular with cyclists.

Route 2

HOLY ISLAND – HOLYHEAD AND SOUTH STACK

Route information

Distance 18km (11 miles)

Grade Moderate

Terrain Although not reaching a great height, this is an undulating route with several steep climbs, particularly on the road to South Stack. Minor roads and 1km (0.6 mile) on the A5.

Time to allow 2–5 hours.

Getting there by car Holyhead is at the north west end of the A5. There is plenty of parking close to the Maritime Museum, the start of the route, except at weekends and at the height of the holiday season.

Getting there by train Holyhead Station is the terminus for the main line from Chester, Crewe and London. A number of train companies operate services to Holyhead. Telephone (0345) 484950 for details.

From Holyhead, with its busy harbour, the route follows quiet country lanes to South Stack and the cliffs and lighthouse. Turning south, the route heads past several groups of ancient circles, Irishmen's Huts or Cytian'r Gwyddelod and prehistoric standing stones. On passing Porth Dafarch, an attractive bay with a sandy beach and extensive views south east along the coast to and beyond Trearddur Bay, followed by a good descent to Trearddur itself. The route then returns to Holyhead by a narrow lane, passing more standing stones and a burial chamber.

Places of interest along the route

A Holyhead

Holyhead is not situated on Anglesey, as most people think, but on Holy Island which lies to the north west of Anglesey, connected by the Stanley Embankement and Four Mile Bridge. The **Maritime Museum**, located in the old lifeboat house, describes the town's history and its links with the sea. The 2.5km (1.5 mile) long breakwater was constructed in the 19th century from stone quarried nearby on a site which is now **Breakwater Country Park**. The park contains tarmac roads where cycling is allowed, and there are interesting information boards describing the construction of the breakwater. Telephone the town's Tourist Information Centre for further information on (01407) 762622.

B Irishmen's Huts (Cytian'r Gwyddelod)

There are several such groups of stone hut circles (believed to have been occupied between the 2nd and 4th centuries AD), and Iron and Bronze Age forts on Holy Island. They are generally clearly signposted and described by information boards. Free access at all reasonable times.

C Ellin's Tower RSPB Seabird Centre, Gogarth Bay

The centre is set on South Stack, high about the lighthouse. Live TV pictures allow close-up views of the nesting seabirds. Also observation

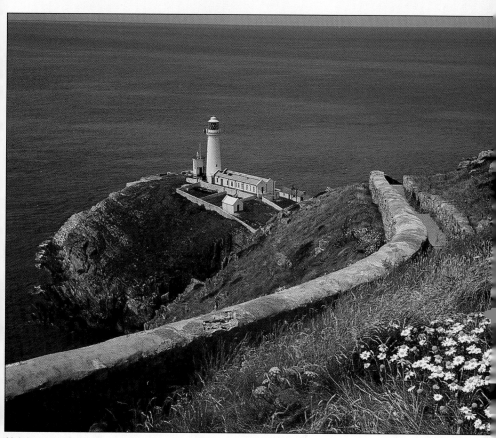

Lighthouse at South Stack

points and clifftop walks. Café. Open Easter to mid-September, daily 1100–1700. Admission free. Telephone (01407) 764973.

D South Stack Lighthouse

Situated on the small island of South Stack, off the coast of Holy Island, the lighthouse is open to visitors. From the end of the tarmac road, descend the zig zag path of approximately 400 steps to cross the bridge. Open Easter to September, daily 1100–1700. Charge (obtain tickets from the café).

E Trearddur Bay

A popular holiday resort which can be busy during the holiday season. There are several sandy beaches, with facilities for sailing, canoeing, water skiing and scuba diving. Telephone Holyhead Tourist Information Centre for further information.

Food and drink

Plenty of choice in Holyhead and Trearddur.

Ellin's Tower RSPB Seabird Centre, Gogarth Bay
A purpose built café.

N
Holyhead Bay
Breakwater
North Stack
Porth Namarch
New Harbour
Porth Penrhyn-mawr
Maritime Museum
Salt Island
Gogarth Bay
Holyhead Mountain
150
100
Llaingoch
1
9
South Stack
South Stack Lighthouse D
Irishmen's Huts B
Tŵr
Holyhead (Caergybi) A
Nimrod Rocks
Traeth y Gribin
Penrhos
Ellin's Tower C
Pen-las Rock
Pen-y-banc
50
8
6
A5
2
3
7
Kingsland
Beddmanarch Bay
Gors-goch
Holy Island (Ynys Gybi)
Newlands Park
Penrhosfeilw
Penrhyn Mawr
Isallt Bach
5
Valley
Porth Dafarch
Trearddur
4
B4545
Trearddur Bay E
Porth Diana
Glan-traeth
Four Mile Bridge
Scale
0 | Mile
0 | Km

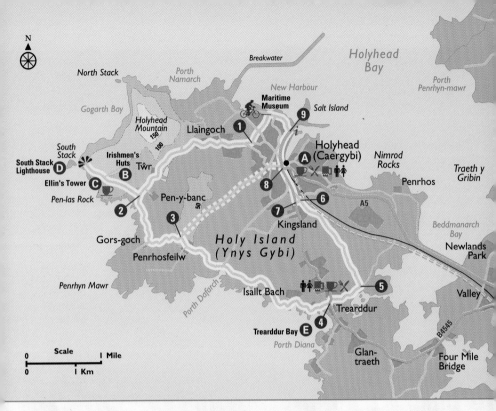

Route description 

Start from the Maritime Museum and TL at mini roundabout into Walthew Avenue, SP South Stack (SP are erected by the RSPB and carry the society's logo). Continue SO at XR into New Park Road.

1 TR at TR, SP South Stack, and continue on this road across the island.

2 TR, SP South Stack/No Through Road. After visiting South Stack, retrace route and TR at TJ, SP Trearddur. ***6.5km (4 miles)***

3 SO at top of short, steep rise (by two seats and where lane goes off to left – if you wish to shorten the route, follow this lane back to Holyhead). Otherwise, continue towards Trearddur Bay.

4 TL at TJ onto B4545, SP Holyhead, for 100m (12km/7.5 miles). TR into Lon Towyn Capel, no SP.

5 TL (SO SP No Through Road). Continue along this road towards Holyhead.

6 TL (SO SP No Through Road).

7 TR onto B4545. ***15km (9.5 miles***

8 Join A5 beside railway and follow brown SP Country Park.

9 TL and follow SP Country Park to Maritime Museum and the end of the ride.

18km (11 miles

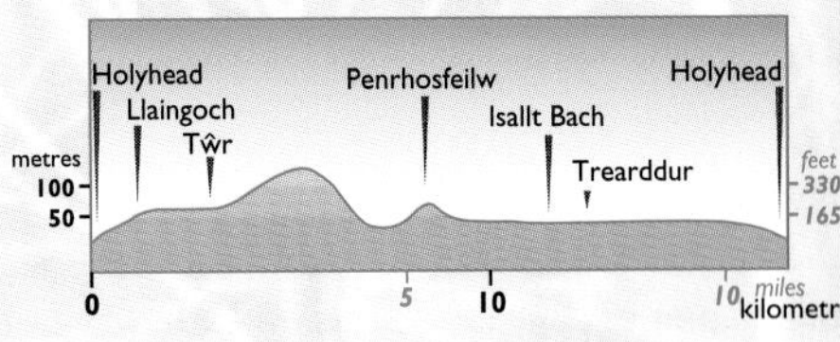

Route 3

BALA LAKE LOOP

Route information

Distance 18.5km (11.5 miles)

Grade Moderate

Terrain On-road, following the A494 (which is not generally busy, particularly out of the main holiday season). The return is along a quiet B road. There are several climbs, but nothing severe.

Time to allow 2–3 hours.

Getting there by car Bala is on the A494 Corwen to Dolgellau road, approximately 14km (8.5 miles) from the A5. There is a car park near the leisure centre at the Bala end of the lake, 1km (0.6 mile) from the town centre.

Getting there by train There is no practical railway access to this ride.

A circuit of Bala Lake (Llyn Tegid), which is located in a beautiful valley between the Cambrian Mountains and Snowdonia National Park. The return route runs alongside a narrow gauge railway.

Places of interest along the route

A Bala

Bala is a market town with important connections with Welsh culture and history. Roman and Norman remains have been found in the town, but the principal claim to fame lies in the importance of its woollen industry during the 18th century. Today the town is popular with visitors as a gateway to Snowdonia. **Bala Lake** (Llyn Tegid), Wales' largest natural lake, is home to a wide range of wildlife including otters and the Gwyniad, a unique species of fish related to the herring and found only in this lake. The lake is a magnificent setting for watersports, especially dinghy sailing; many national and international class championships have been held here. For further information telephone Bala Tourist Information Centre on (01678) 521021.

B Bala Lake Railway

A narrow gauge line that runs along the eastern shore of the lake between Bala and Llanuwchllyn. The 14.5km (9 mile) return trip takes about an hour and there are intermediate stops along the way. For details of fares, train times, party bookings and special events telephone (01678) 540666.

Food and drink

There are several teashops and pubs in Bala and a picnic site with public toilets just off the B4403 at Llangower Point.

Loch Café, Bala

At the start of the route. Open between Whitsun and September. There are some interesting old photographs of the area displayed on the walls.

Llanuwchllyn Railway Station

The station's café is open whenever there are trains running.

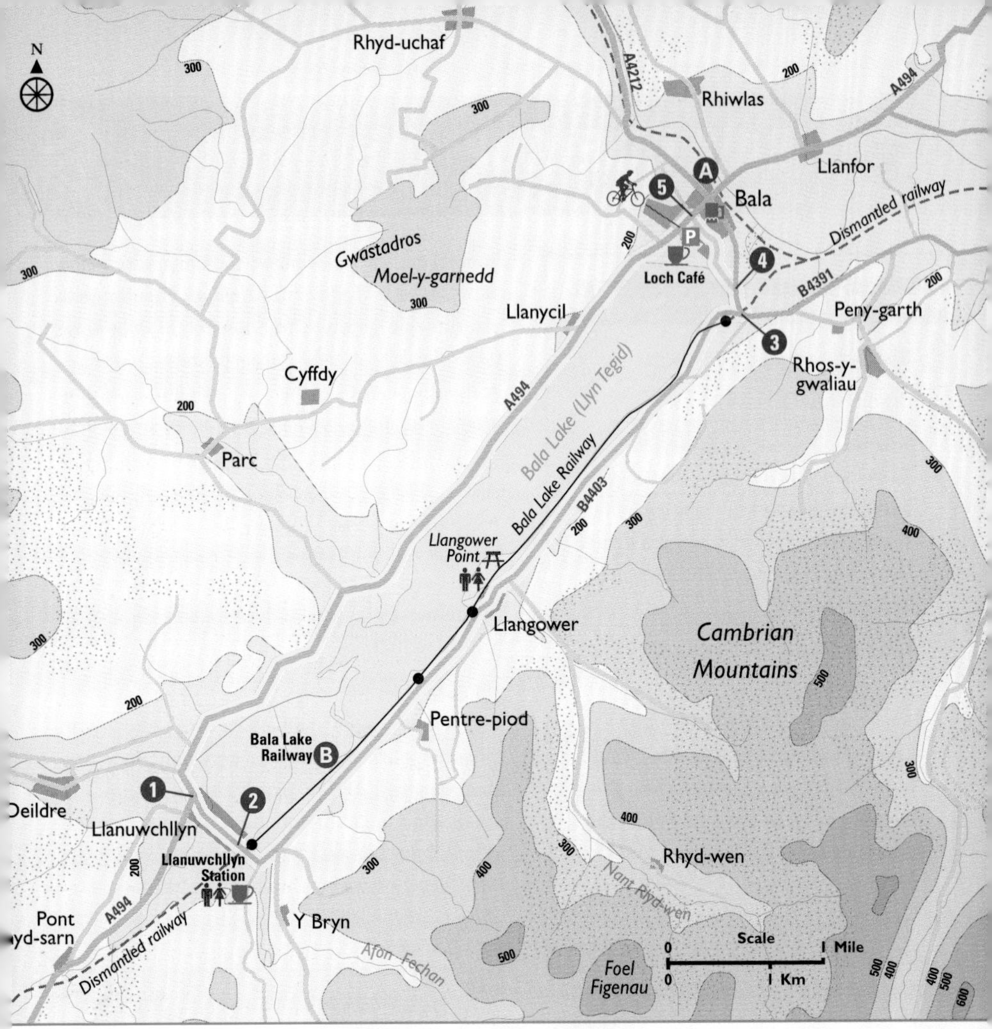

Route description

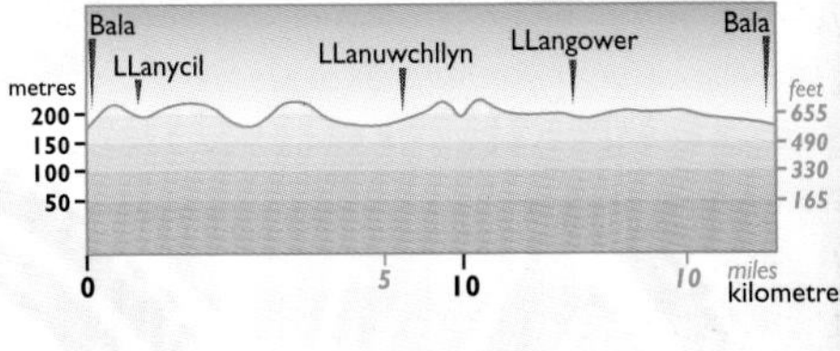

Start from the car park near the leisure centre at the Bala end of the lake. TL out of car park onto A494 and follow this road along the lakeside to Llanuwchllyn.

1 TL opposite petrol station, SP Llangower B4403. ***8km (5 miles)***

2 To visit Llanuwchllyn Station TL, SP Bala Lake Railway. Otherwise, continue and TL at TJ to follow B4403 beside lake. Continue along this road towards Bala, passing picnic area on LHS ***(12.5km/8 miles)***

3 TL at TJ onto B4391, SP Bala.

4 Take first TL, SP Town Centre, and continue into Bala.

5 TL at TJ onto High Street (A494) and follow this road back to the car park and the end of the ride. ***18.5km (11.5 miles)***

Route 4

VALE OF CLWYD – RUTHIN TO LLANGWYFAN

Route information

Distance 20km (12.5 miles)

Grade Easy

Terrain Narrow lanes, uphill for the first 4km (2.5 miles).

Time to allow 2–3 hours.

Getting there by car From the north leave the A55 at St Asaph and follow the A525 to Ruthin. From the south leave the A5 at Llangollen and follow the A542 and then the A525 to Ruthin. There is a car park at Ruthin Craft Centre.

Getting there by train There is no practical railway access to this ride. The nearest railway station is at Rhyl, 29km (18 miles) away.

From Ruthin in the Vale of Clwyd, along the western flank of the Clwydian Hills, a designated Area of Outstanding Natural Beauty. Following narrow lanes the route heads uphill to Hirwaen and then along a level road to Llangwyfan before turning south back to Ruthin.

Places of interest along the route

A Ruthin

The old market town of Ruthin, situated beside the River Clwyd, has been a local administrative centre for over 700 years. The town retains its medieval street plan, with the 14th-century St Peters Church at its centre. Together with many other medieval buildings, visitors can see Elizabethan town houses, a 16th-century half-timbered coaching inn and fine 18th- and 19th-century civic buildings. The Tourist Information Centre can supply a free leaflet describing all the main buildings – telephone (01824) 703992. **Ruthin Craft Centre**, Park Road, contains several craft studios and displays a wide range of contemporary applied art from all over the country. Also restaurant. Centre open June to September, daily 1000–1730; October to May, Monday–Saturday 1000–1700, Sunday 1200–1700. Studio opening times vary. Telephone the Tourist Information Centre for more details.

B Llangwyfan Church, Llangwyfan

Typical of village churches in the Vale of Clwyd, but with an unusual feature in the presence of stocks adjacent to the churchyard gates. There are splendid views from the churchyard.

Food and drink

Ruthin has a number of cafés and pubs and the restaurant at the Craft Centre.

Golden Lion, Llangynhafal
Pub serving meals.

Kinmel Arms, Waen
Bar meals available. Children's playground.

White Horse Inn, Hendrerwydd
Bar meals served.

Route description 

TR out of Ruthin Craft Centre car park for 100m, then TL at roundabout. Almost immediately, TL at TJ, no SP. Continue out of Ruthin and along this road.

1 SO at XR, SP Hirwaen.

2 TL at TJ opposite telephone box, no SP (4km/2.5 miles). Continue into Llangynhafal.

3 In Llangynhafal take RHF by Golden Lion pub, SP Llangwyfan. Continue into Rhibwbebyll.

4 To visit Llangwyfan Church, SO at XR (opposite large stone bus shelter) for 0.5km (0.3 mile). After visit retrace to XR where TR to rejoin route.

Otherwise, TL at XR , SP Llandyrnog.

5 To visit Kinmel Arms Hotel, TR at XR, SP Denbigh. Otherwise, TL at XR, SP Hendrerwydd/Llangynhafal.

6 Take RHF, SP Hendrerwydd. Continue into Hendrerwydd.

7 SO at XR by pub, SP Gellifor/Llanbedr D.C.

8 TL (apparent SO) onto B5429, SP Llanbedr D.C. (15.5km/9.5 miles). Continue and pass bungalows on LHS.

9 TR at XR (immediately after passing bungalows). Continue into Ruthin.

10 TR at traffic island and then TR at roundabout, following SP Ruthin Craft Centre to finish the ride. ***20km (12.5 miles)***

Vale of Clwyd

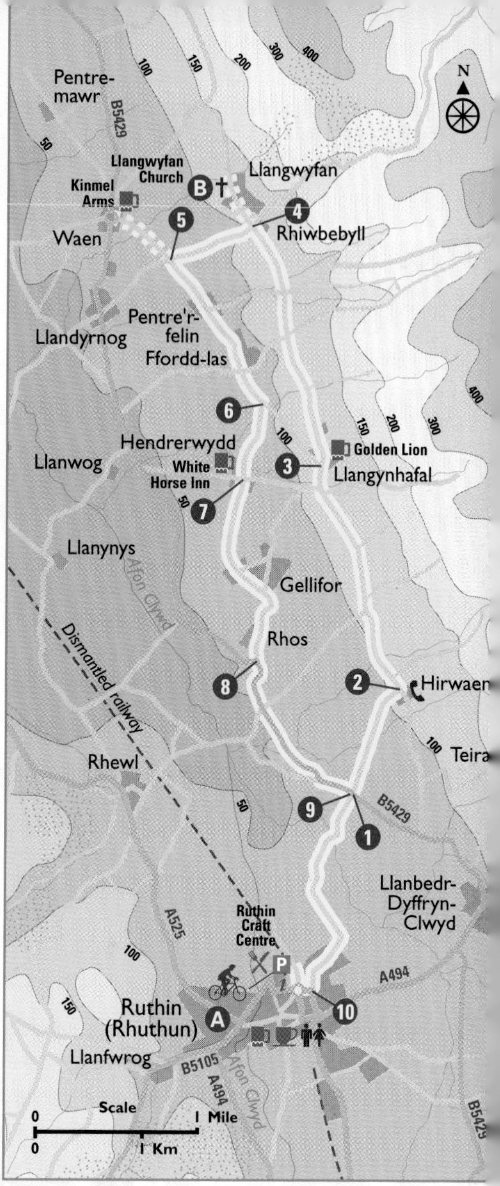

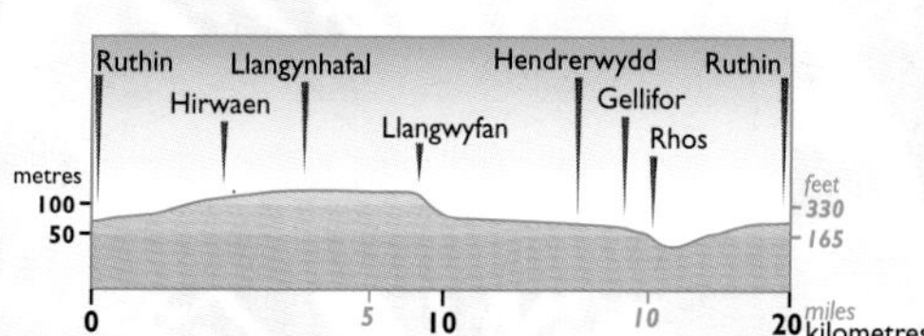

Route 5

CAERNARFON AND GLYNLLIFON COUNTRY PARK

Route information

Distance 22.5km (14 miles)

Grade Easy

Terrain Mostly flat country lanes and designated cycleway.

Time to allow 2–3 hours.

Getting there by car Caernarfon is reached from the A55 and the A487. Park at Victoria Dock (near Safeway supermarket).

Getting there by train There is no practical rail access to this route.

From Caernarfon, via the footbridge opposite the castle, the route runs alongside the Menai Strait before turning inland along country lanes heading south to Glynllifon Country Park. An optional extension (approximately 4.5km/3 miles) takes you to the Welsh Highland Railway and the Air World Museum at Dinas. The final section of the route uses the Lôn Eifion Cycleway, which runs alongside the railway back to Caernarfon.

Places of interest along the route

A Caernarfon

The walled town of Caernarfon is dominated by its **castle**, built by Edward I as a military stronghold, seat of government and a royal palace. In 1969 the castle was used as the setting for the investiture of Prince Charles as Prince of Wales. Together with exhibitions on its history, the castle contains the Royal Welch Fusiliers Museum. Cadw (Welsh Historic Monuments) property. Open daily, end March to May and October 0930–1700; end May to September 0930–1800; November to March 0930–1600. Charge. Telephone (01286) 677617.

B Caernarfon Airworld, Dinas Dinlle

Originally the site of RAF Llandwrog in 1940, today the airfield houses an air museum displaying planes and helicopters in landscaped sites, over 400 model aircraft and various exhibitions. Pleasure flights of between 10 and 40 minutes duration are offered. Café open all year. Museum open March to November, daily 0900–1730. Pleasure flights operate daily throughout the year, weather permitting. Charge. Telephone (01286) 830800.

C Glynllifon Country Park

The park contains an exhibition describing life on a country estate and has its own gas works, used to provide lighting for the estate. Café. Free access at all reasonable times. Telephone

Menai Strait

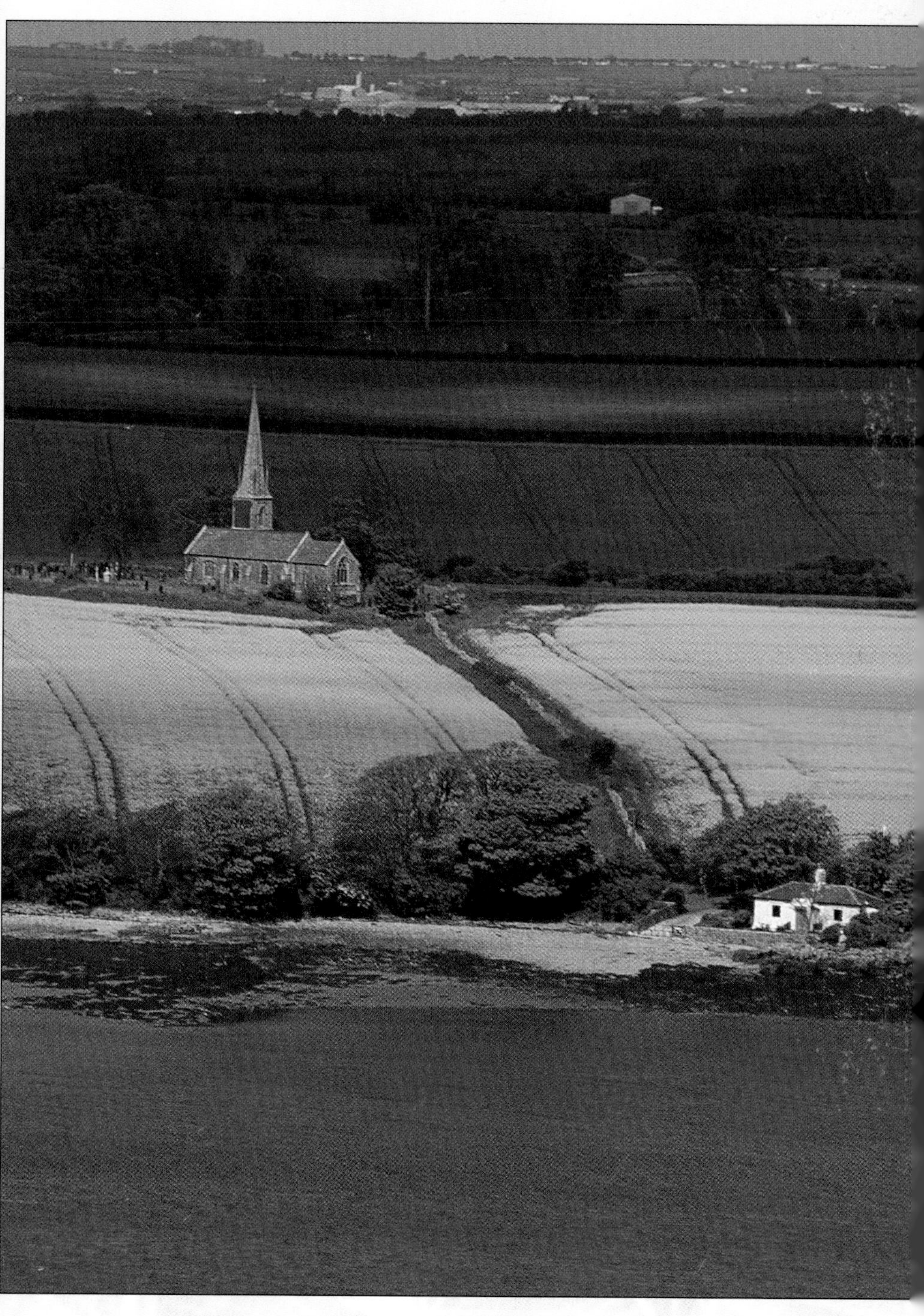

Caernarfon Tourist Information Centre for information on (01286) 672232.

D West Highland Railway

The railway is operated by the Ffestiniog Railway Company and at present runs between Caernarfon and Dinas. Steam trains take passengers through the gentle countryside with magnificent views of the Menai Strait. Telephone (01766) 512340 for further information. Bicycles are carried on some trains but you should telephone in advance to confirm.

Route description

Start from the car park at Victoria Dock. Follow the road south, keeping to the edge of the straits around the town walls, and cross the footbridge opposite the castle.

1 TR and follow road along edge of straits for approximately 4.5km (3 miles) and then follow it inland.

2 TR at TJ (6.5km/4 miles), descend, cross bridge and follow road through Saron into Llandwrog.

3 To visit Caernarfon Airworld TR at TJ (opposite Harp Hotel) and follow SP Dinas Dinlle/Caernarfon Airport. After visit retrace route to Harp Hotel, where TR and continue to A499.

Otherwise, TL at TJ opposite Harp Hotel and continue to A499.

4 TR WITH CARE at TJ, SP Pwllheli. Then TL to Glynllifon Park.

5 After visit TR WITH CARE onto A499. Then TL at first junction, SP Llandwrog, and return to village.

6 TR at junction (immediately before church gate) onto single track road.

12.5km (8 miles)

7 TL at junction.

8 TR at TJ. Continue through Saron (do NOT TL to sea shore) and Llanfaglan to narrow gauge railway. ***(17.5km/11 miles).***

9 Road meets narrow gauge railway – cross track onto Lôn Eifion Cycleway. TR and follow cycleway to Caernarfon. TR onto road and continue alongside shore back to Victoria Dock to finish the ride.

22.5km (14 miles)

Food and drink

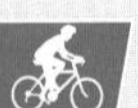

There are plenty of places offering refreshment in Caernarfon and Dinas Dinlle. Glynllifon Country Park (open Easter to September) and Caernarfon Airworld also have cafés.

Harp Hotel, Llandwrog

Bar meals available.

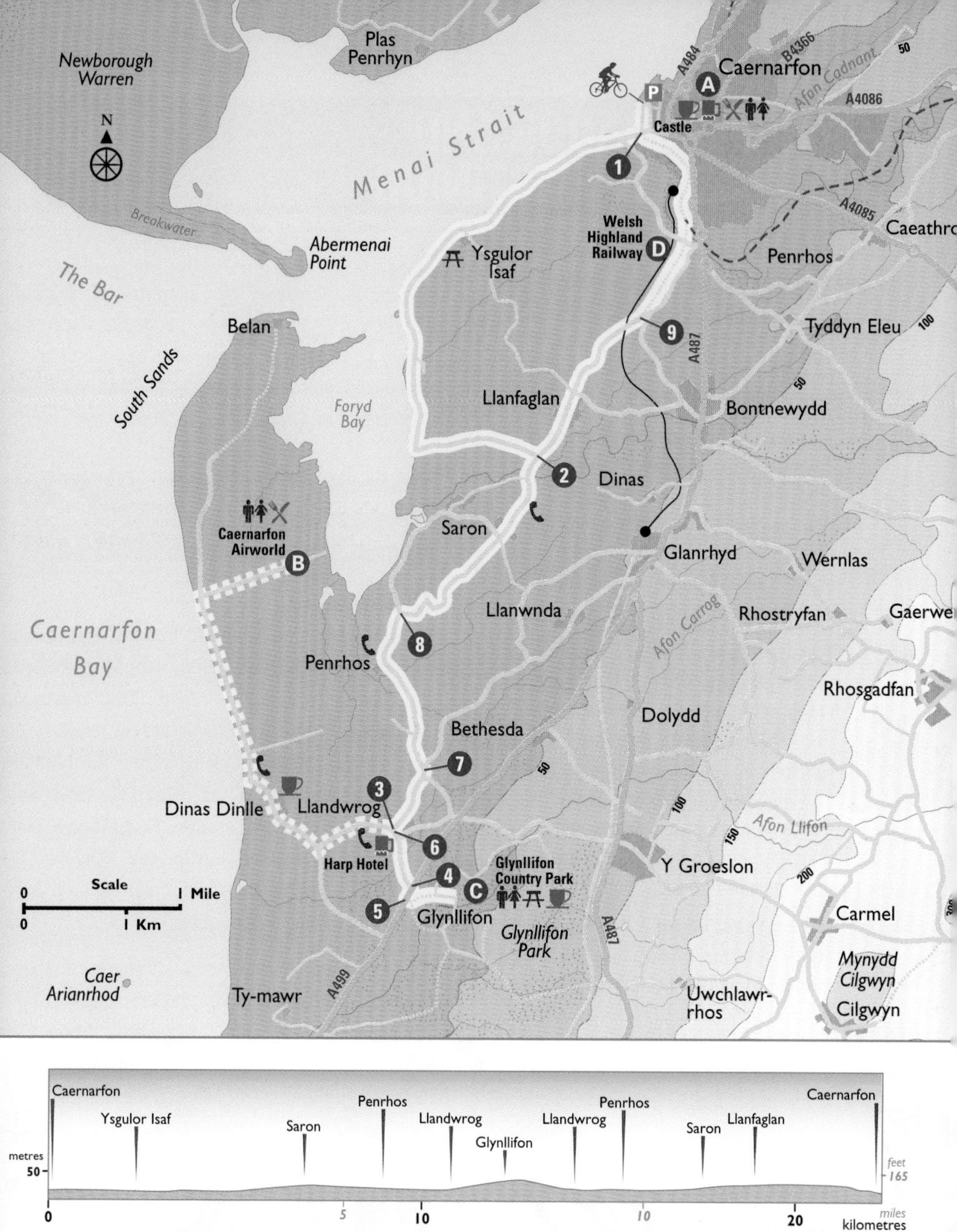

Newborough Warren
Plas Penrhyn
Menai Strait
N
Breakwater
Abermenai Point
The Bar
Belan
South Sands
Foryd Bay
Caernarfon
A484
B4366
Afon Cadnant
A4086
50
Castle
A
1
Welsh Highland Railway
D
A4085
Caeathro
Penrhos
Ysgulor Isaf
9
A487
Tyddyn Eleu
100
50
Llanfaglan
Bontnewydd
2
Dinas
Caernarfon Airworld
B
Saron
Glanrhyd
Wernlas
Llanwnda
Afon Carrog
Rhostryfan
Gaerwe
Caernarfon Bay
8
Penrhos
Rhosgadfan
Bethesda
Dolydd
7
50
3
Dinas Dinlle
Llandwrog
100
Afon Llifon
150
6
Harp Hotel
Y Groeslon
200
Scale
0
1 Mile
0
1 Km
4
Glynllifon Country Park
C
5
Glynllifon
Carmel
Glynllifon Park
A487
Mynydd Cilgwyn
Caer Arianrhod
Ty-mawr
A499
Uwchlawr-rhos
Cilgwyn
Caernarfon
Ysgulor Isaf
Saron
Penrhos
Llandwrog
Glynllifon
Llandwrog
Penrhos
Saron
Llanfaglan
Caernarfon
metres
50
feet
165
0
5
10
10
20
miles
kilometres

Route 6

PORTHMADOG AND BLAENAU FFESTINIOG

Route information

Distance 24km (15 miles)

Grade Moderate

Terrain Rugged terrain but the route uses the Ffestiniog Mountain Railway uphill between Porthmadog and Blaenau Ffestiniog, so the cycling is for the most part downhill, with three short, steep hills for which low gears will be useful.

Time to allow The train journey from Porthmadog to Blaenau Ffestiniog takes about an hour and the cycle ride directly back to Porthmadog is a further 2 hours at most. However, if you visit the slate quarry and/or the power station, and it would be a shame to miss either of them, the entire trip could take most of the day.

Getting there by car Porthmadog is on the A487 and A497. Once in Porthmadog, the station for the Ffestiniog Mountain Railway is by the harbour at the south end of town, where there is parking. The station is signposted, but do not confuse the Ffestiniog Mountain Railway with the Welsh Highland Line – they are at opposite ends of town.

Getting there by train There is a mainline station at Porthmadog (close to the Welsh Highland Line). Leave the mainline station car park, TR and follow SP along main street to the Ffestiniog Mountain Railway. For information on mainline train travel telephone (0345) 484950.

From Porthmadog the route uses the Ffestiniog Mountain Railway to ascend to Blaenau Ffestiniog. From here you follow the road back down to Porthmadog and the Glaslyn Estuary. There are glorious views up the estuary to the mountains of Snowdonia National Park.

Places of interest along the route

A Porthmadog

Porthmadog is a popular holiday destination with a small harbour from where slate was shipped all over the world. The **Ffestiniog Mountain Railway** features steam hauled narrow gauge trains which run from Porthmadog into the mountains at Blaenau Ffestiniog. There is a café at the station. Telephone (01766) 512340 for train times and prices. Bicycles are carried on many trains, but you should telephone in advance to confirm.

B Llechwedd Slate Caverns, Blaenau Ffestiniog

Visitors can tour the spectacular underground caverns via two rides: the Deep Mine tour offers a 25-minute walk through a *son et lumière* sequence; the Miners Tramway carries visitors through a network of man-made caverns constructed in 1846. Also recreated Victorian village, and a café, pub and restaurant. Open all year, daily from 1000; March to September last tours at 1715; October to February last tours at 1615. Charge. Telephone (0800) 252914.

C Ffestiniog Power Station Visitor Centre, near Blaenau Ffestiniog

The visitor centre describes the development of the country's first pumped storage hydroelectric power station through interactive displays, an audio-visual presentation and a subterranean tour through the power station itself. Visitors can also see the upper reservoir and dam at Stwlan (magnificent views from here). Café and picnic areas. Open Easter to October. Charge. Telephone (01766) 830465 for tour times and availability.

Although not passed on the route, the mock Italianate village of **Portmeirion** is only 3km (2 miles) from Porthmadog, SP from the A487 (a busy road). The village was made famous as the location of the 1960s cult television series *The Prisoner*. Restaurant, ice cream parlour and gift shop. Village and gardens open all year, daily 0930–1730. Charge. Telephone (01766) 770000.

Ffestiniog Railway, Porthmadog

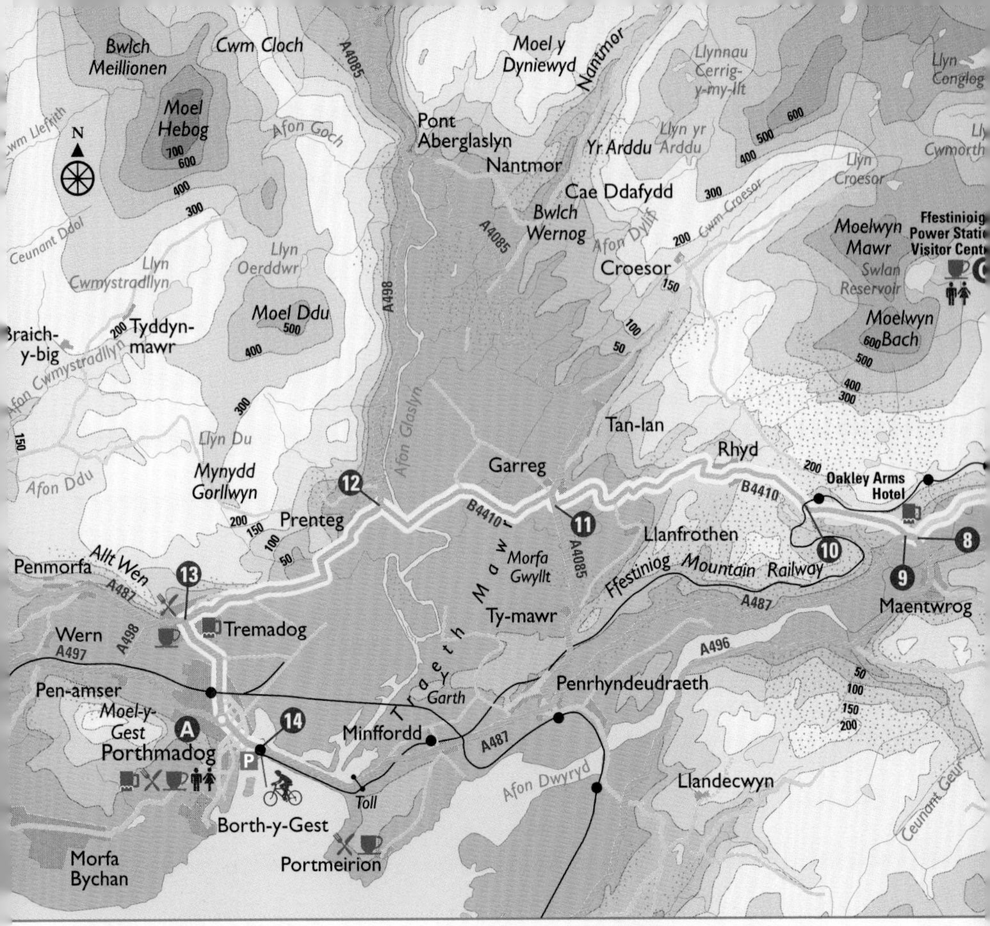

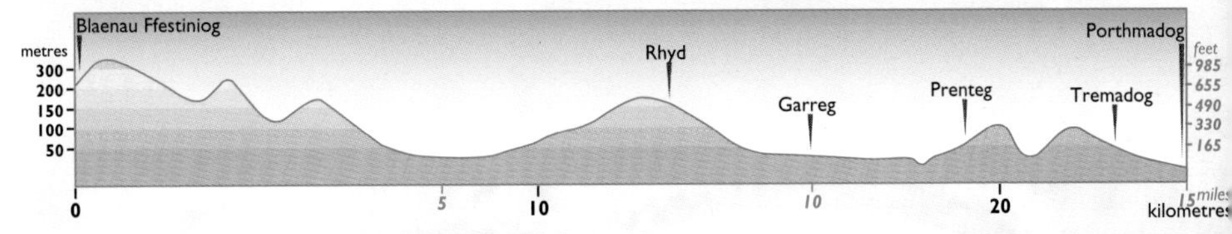

Route description

Take the Ffestiniog Mountain Railway from Porthmadog to Blaenau Ffestiniog.

1 TL out of Blaenau Ffestiniog station car park, no SP.

2 To visit the Slate Caverns TR at roundabout, SP Betws-y-coed. The caverns are approximately 1.5km (1 mile) up a fairly steep hill on RHS. Take care on this road as it is frequently used by lorries. After visit retrace to roundabout at Blaenau Ffestiniog where TR and continue to direction 3.

Otherwise, TL at roundabout, SP Porthmadog/Dolgellau/Bala.

3 Arrive LH bend. TR WITH CARE onto unclassified road, SP Workshops. Keep L immediately after level crossing.

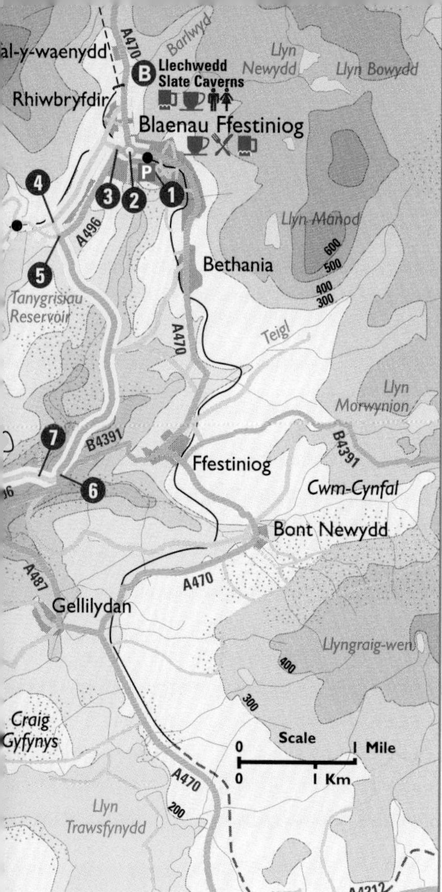

4 TL by SP No Through Road/ Maentwrog/train symbol. ***2.5km (1.5 miles)***

5 Arrive junction with A496. To visit Ffestiniog Power Station Visitor Centre take sharp TR at TJ. After visit retrace to junction, TR onto A496, SP Maentwrog, and descend to direction 6.

Otherwise, TR onto A496, SP Maentwrog. You are now at the start of a long and at times steep descent. Follow road downhill.

6 Easy to miss – TR onto unclassified road, immediately before TJ with main road, by SP Width Restriction (6.5km/4 miles). Beware – the surface on this minor road is good, but there are many loose pebbles and gravel as well as the occasional stray sheep. Continue across narrow bridge.

7 TL immediately after narrow bridge, no SP.

8 TR at TJ onto A487, no SP.

9 TR onto B4410 (by Oakley Arms Hotel), SP Rhyd (10km/6 miles). Continue for three short, steepish hills in fairly quick succession – the first one is the hardest.

10 Pass under railway bridge and continue along B4410.

11 TR and immediately TL onto B4410, SP Prenteg/Tremadog. ***16km (10 miles)***

12 TL at TJ, SP Porthmadog.

13 TL, SP Porthmadog. Continue along main street, following SP Ffestiniog Mountain Railway Station. SO at roundabout in town centre.

14 TR into car park by station to finish the ride. ***24km (15 miles)***

Food and drink

Plenty of choice in Porthmadog, Blaenau Ffestiniog and Tremadog. Refreshments are also available at the Ffestiniog Mountain Railway station at Porthmadog, Llechwedd Slate Caverns and Ffestiniog Power Station Visitor Centre.

Oakley Arms Hotel, Maentwrog
Half-way along the ride, offering bar meals.

Route 7

LLANFAIRPWLLGWYNGYLL AND BRYNSIENCYN

Route information

Distance 25.5km (16 miles)

Grade Easy

Terrain Mostly flat, quiet country lanes. The A road used is not usually busy.

Time to allow 3–4 hours.

Getting there by car Llanfairpwll is just off the A5 on the Anglesey side of Britannia Bridge across the Menai Strait. Park at the railway station.

Getting there by train The railway station is on the main London/ Chester/Holyhead line. Telephone (0345) 484950 for travel details.

This route takes in a small corner of Anglesey. From Llanfairpwll the route heads south west to Brynsiencyn, offering great views of the Menai Strait along the way. On north west to Maesoglen, before turning north east for the ride back to Llanfairpwll along pleasant country lanes.

Places of interest along the route

A Llanfairpwllgwyngyll

The town's railway station dates from 1848 and was the first on Anglesey. It is well-known for having the longest name of any station in the country. Beside the station is **James Pringle Weavers Visitor Centre**, with two 15" gauge Atlantic Class steam locomotives, sales of knitwear, a café and Tourist Information Centre. Open all year, daily. Telephone (01248) 713177 for further information. The **Marquis of Anglesey's Column** was completed in 1815 and the statue added in 1860 to commemorate his bravery at the Battle of Waterloo. Visitors can climb the internal staircase for spectacular views of the Snowdonia mountains and the Menai Strait. Also garden and café. Open all year, daily 0900–1700 (October to May closed Wednesday). Nominal charge. **Pilas Palas Butterfly Palace** is 2.5km (1.5 miles) outside Llanfairpwll on the A5025. The tropical butterfly house contains hundreds of butterflies from all over the world. Also exotic birds, snakes, spiders and lizards. Shop and café. Open daily, March to October 1000–1730; November and December 1100–1530. Charge. Telephone (01248) 712474.

B Sea Zoo, Brynsiencyn

The Sea Zoo contains large scale displays of all sorts of sea creatures including rays, sea urchins, starfish, seahorses and conger eels. Hands-on displays. Gift and coffee shop (access free). Open all year, summer daily 1000–1800; telephone to confirm winter opening times. Charge. Telephone (01248) 430411.

C Foel Farm Park, Brynsiencyn

A working farm home to dozens of animals. Visitors can feed and touch many of them, or help with the milking. The tearoom sells home-made ice cream. Open March to October, daily 1030–1730; November to February, weekends only. Charge. Telephone (01248) 430646.

Ⓓ Plas Newydd, near Llanfairpwll

An impressive 18th-century house in unspoilt gardens alongside the Menai Strait. The house contains Rex Whistler's largest wall painting and a military museum. Also woodland and marine walk and cruises (weather permitting). National Trust property. Café. Open March to October, Saturday–Wednesday: garden 1100–1730; house 1200–1700. Charge. Telephone (01248) 714795.

Two neolithic burial chambers are also passed en route – Bodowyr and Bryn Celli Ddu.

Food and drink

Plenty of choice for pub meals in Llanfairpwll. Refreshments are also available at James Pringle Weavers, the Sea Zoo, Foel Farm Park and Plas Newydd.

The Groeslon, Brynsiencyn
Bar meals offered.

Mermaid Inn, Menai Strait
Pub food available.

Route description

TL out of station car park in Llanfairpwll and cycle to end of village.

1 TL into lane (90m before A5 dual carriageway) and go over railway bridge.

2 TR at TJ onto A4080. Continue on A4080 to Brynsiencyn.

3 SO at junction (opposite Groeslon pub – main road goes right), SP Foel Farm Park/Sea Zoo. Follow lane down to water's edge and continue to Sea Zoo and Farm Park.

7 km (4.5 miles)

4 TR onto B4419, SP A4080.

5 TR at TJ onto A4080.

6 TL at junction onto B4419, SP Llangaffo/Dwyran.

7 SO at XR.

8 TR at junction, SP Cycle Route 8. Pass Bodowyr burial chamber on LHS.

Llanfairpwllgwyngyll railway station

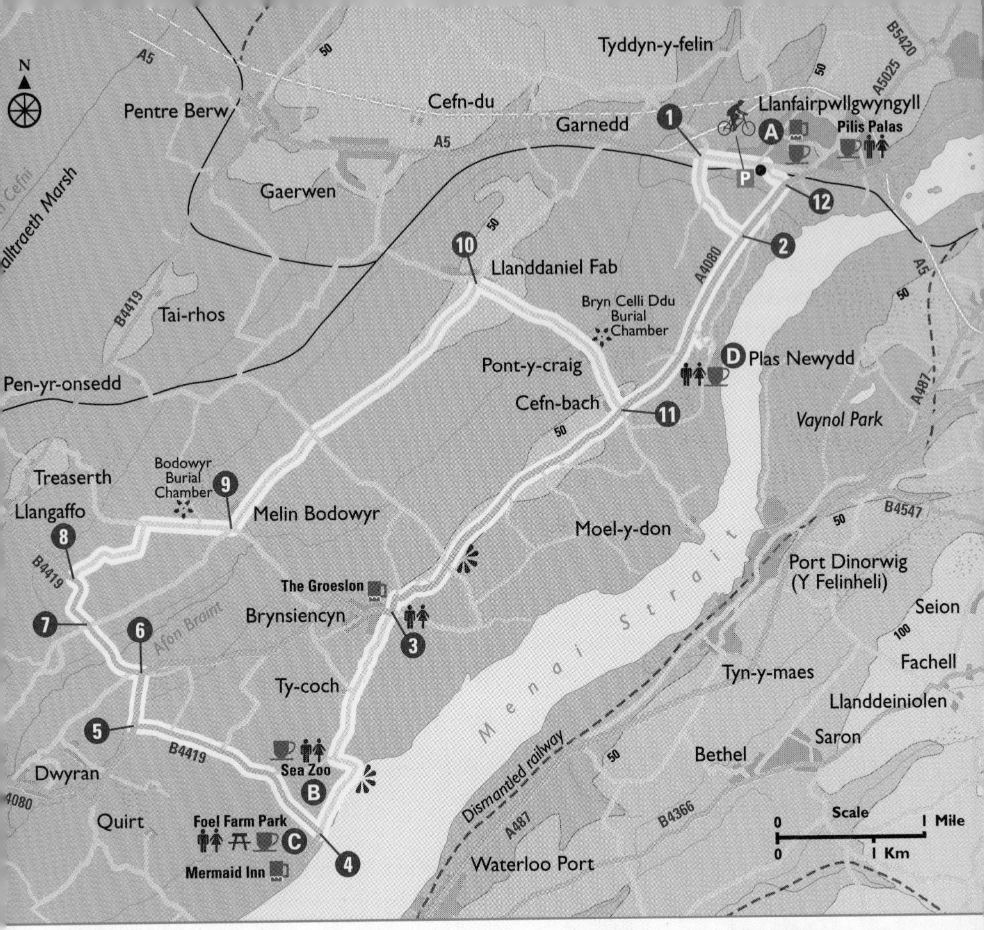

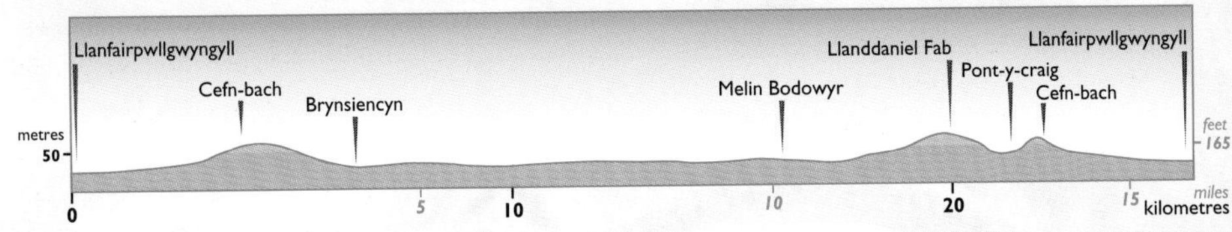

9 TL at XR. Continue on this road to Llanddaniel Fab. ***16km (10 miles)***

10 TR at XR, SP Llanedwen/Bryn Celli Ddu. Pass Bryn Celli Ddu burial chamber on LHS (opposite school).

11 TL at XR onto A4080, SP Llanfairpwll. Pass Plas Newydd on RHS. Continue on A4080 into Llanfairpwll.

12 Road dips at end of long stone wall – TL at junction after SP 30mph, over level crossing, and TL at TJ to return to station car park and complete the route.

25.5 km (16 miles)

Route **8**

WELSHPOOL AND THE LONG MOUNTAIN

Route information

Distance 26 km (16 miles)

Grade Strenuous

Terrain The Long Mountain is steep sided and suitable only for bicycles with low gears.

Time to allow 3–4 hours.

Getting there by car Welshpool is on the A483 Chester to Newtown road and can also be reached from Shrewsbury via the A458. There is plenty of car parking in the town.

Getting there by train There is a mainline station in Welshpool. Telephone (0345) 484950 for travel information. Leave the station via the footbridge which places you outside the Old Station, now converted into shops and a café and the start of the ride.

From Welshpool this route climbs up the Long Mountain, traverses the top following an old Roman road, descends part of the way down and then follows a road around the north side of the hill, before dropping back into the Severn Valley. Apart from the superb views, you stand a good chance of seeing buzzards and maybe even a red kite.

Places of interest along the route

Ⓐ Welshpool

Welshpool is a small market town with many half-timbered buildings, characteristic of the Upper Severn Valley. The town sits by the **Montgomery Canal**. Visitors can take a narrow boat trip or hire a self-drive boat. Trips operate April to October, daily. Charge. Telephone for details of times on (01938) 553271. The **Old Station**, designed in the style of a French chateau, contains a selection of gift shops and a café. Open all year, Monday–Saturday 0900–1745, Sunday 1100–1700. Admission free. Telephone (01938) 556622. The **Welshpool and Llanfair Railway** runs steam hauled trains through the picturesque countryside between Welshpool and Llanfair Caereinion. Special events held throughout the year. Trains run April to October and December. Telephone (01938) 810441 for details. Just south of the town is medieval **Powis Castle**, originally built as a fortress by the Welsh princes. The castle is surrounded by a magnificent garden. National Trust property. Tearoom. Castle open 1300–1700, garden open 1100–1800: March to June, September and October, Wednesday–Sunday; July and August, Tuesday–Sunday and Bank Holidays. Telephone (01938) 557018.

Half-way through the route you will pass Rodney's Pillar. This was erected by 'The Gentlemen of Montgomeryshire' in honour of Admiral Rodney's victory over the French at the Battle of the Sainte's Passage in the West Indies in 1782.

Route description

From whichever car park you use, follow SP Main Line Station to outskirts of Welshpool. Start in front of Old Station and TL onto B4381, SP Leighton.

1 TR at roundabout, SP Leighton. Continue on B4381, crossing River Severn.

2 TR onto B4388, SP Leighton.

3 TL uphill by school, SP Trelystan/Marton.

4 TL by church – do not go ahead into Leighton. This is the start of a very steep hill approximately 2.5km (1.5 miles) long. Stop, even if you do not need to, to look back at the superb views into the hills behind Welshpool.

5 TL at XR, SP Westbury (5.5km/3.5 miles). You have now done all of the really hard work – the few hills that remain are relatively benign! Continue on this road, which follows the route

Powis Castle

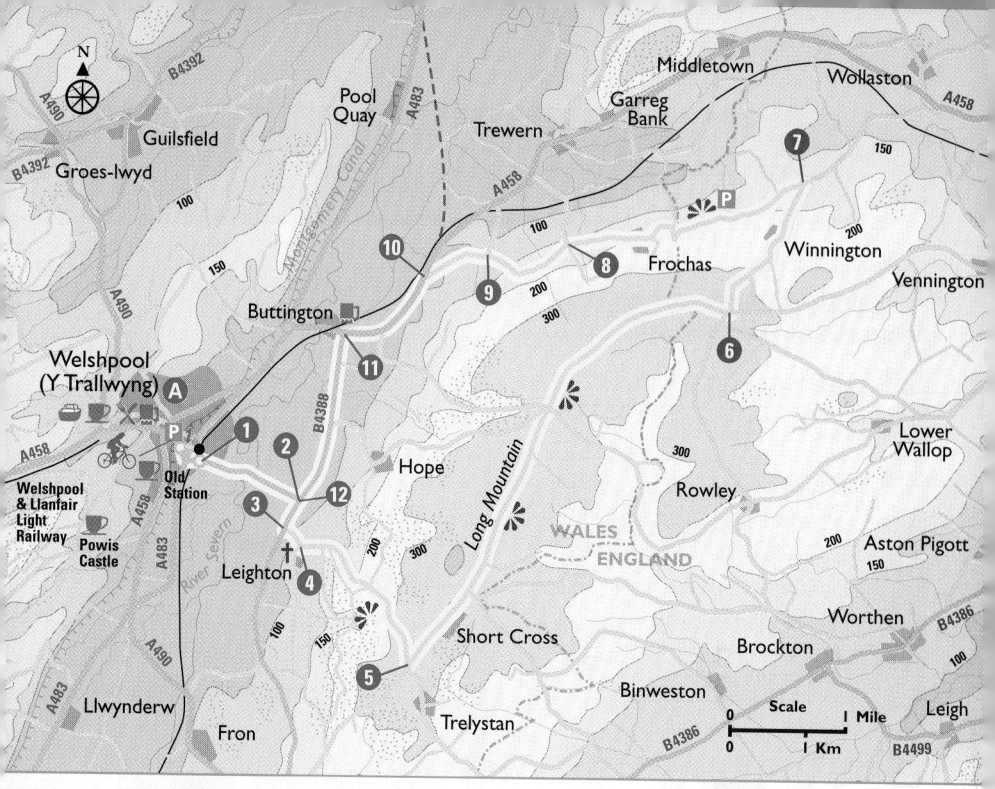

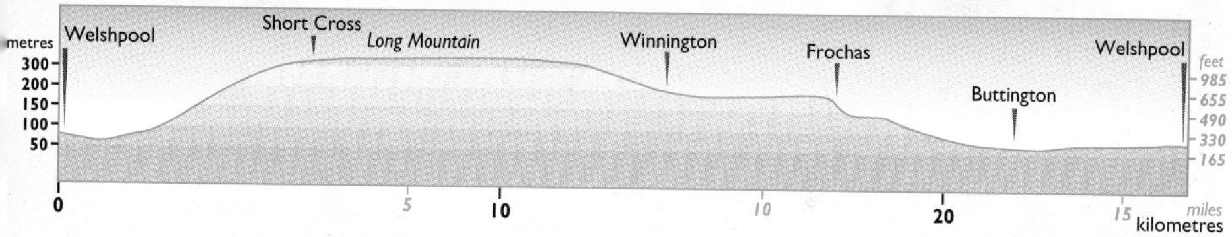

of an old Roman road along the top of the ridge, for tremendous views over the north Shropshire hills.

6 This turn is easy miss as you speed down the hill – TL at XR, SP Winnington.

12.5km (8 miles)

7 TL at TJ, SP Trefnant. Pass Breidden Hills and Rodney's Pillar in the distance on RHS.

8 SO at XR, no SP. ***18.5km (11.5 miles)***

9 Keep L at bottom of hill on sharp bend.

10 TL at TJ with busy A458, no SP.

20.5km (12.5 miles)

11 TL immediately before level crossing, SP Leighton (pub on RHS).

Food and drink

There are plenty of cafés and hotels in Welshpool but none along the route until you reach a pub at Buttington. Refreshments are also available at the Old Station and Powis Castle. You should carry food and drink to sustain you through the ride.

12 TR, SP Welshpool. Recross River Severn and follow SP for Town Centre, arriving back at Old Station to complete the ride.

26km (16 miles)

Route 9

LLANFAIR CAEREINION AND THE RIVER VYRNWY

Route information

Distance 34km (21 miles)

Grade Strenuous

Terrain Undulating, narrow lanes and a quiet A road. Steady climbs with occasional steeper sections, and a steep descent on the return journey to Llanfair Caereinion.

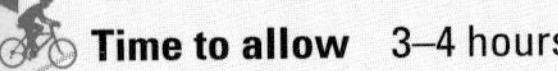

Time to allow 3–4 hours.

Getting there by car Follow the A458 from Welshpool to Llanfair Caereinion. There is car parking at the Welshpool and Llanfair Light Railway Station.

Getting there by train The nearest main line station is at Welshpool. Telephone (0345) 484950 for mainline travel information. You can travel from Welshpool to Llanfair Caereinion via the Welshpool and Llanfair Light Railway. Bicycles are carried but you must book in advance. Telephone (01938) 810441. The light railway station is at the opposite end of Welshpool from the main line station, on the A458 towards Llanfair Caereinion.

From Llanfair Caereinion the route heads east to Pen-y-bont before turning north to Llwydiarth. The return follows the valley of the River Vyrnwy to Dolanog for a descent back to Llanfair Caereinion. The route offers panoramic views of rural Wales and the likelihood of seeing buzzards and red kites.

Route description

Start from Llanfair Caereinion station and TL onto A458. Follow SP Town Centre.

1 TL onto B4385, SP Town Centre/Cefn Coch. Continue, bear right and go through Melin-y-ddol.

2 TR at XR (immediately after caravan park), no SP.

3 SO at XR over A495 onto minor road, no SP. Follow this road and keep left at third TL, no SP and no road markings.

4 TR onto A495 at TJ, no SP (7km/4.5 miles). Continue along A495, through Pen-y-bont.

5 TR onto B4395, SP Llanfyllin/Lake Vyrnwy. Climb, with excellent views. Descend to Pont Llogel and climb again.

6 Take first TR off B4395, no SP (20km/12.5 miles), and continue along this road.

7 TR at TJ onto B4382, no SP. Continue through Dolanog, passing access to River Vyrnwy weir on LHS after village.

8 TR at grass triangle, no SP (26.5km/16.5 miles). Then take first TL, no SP.

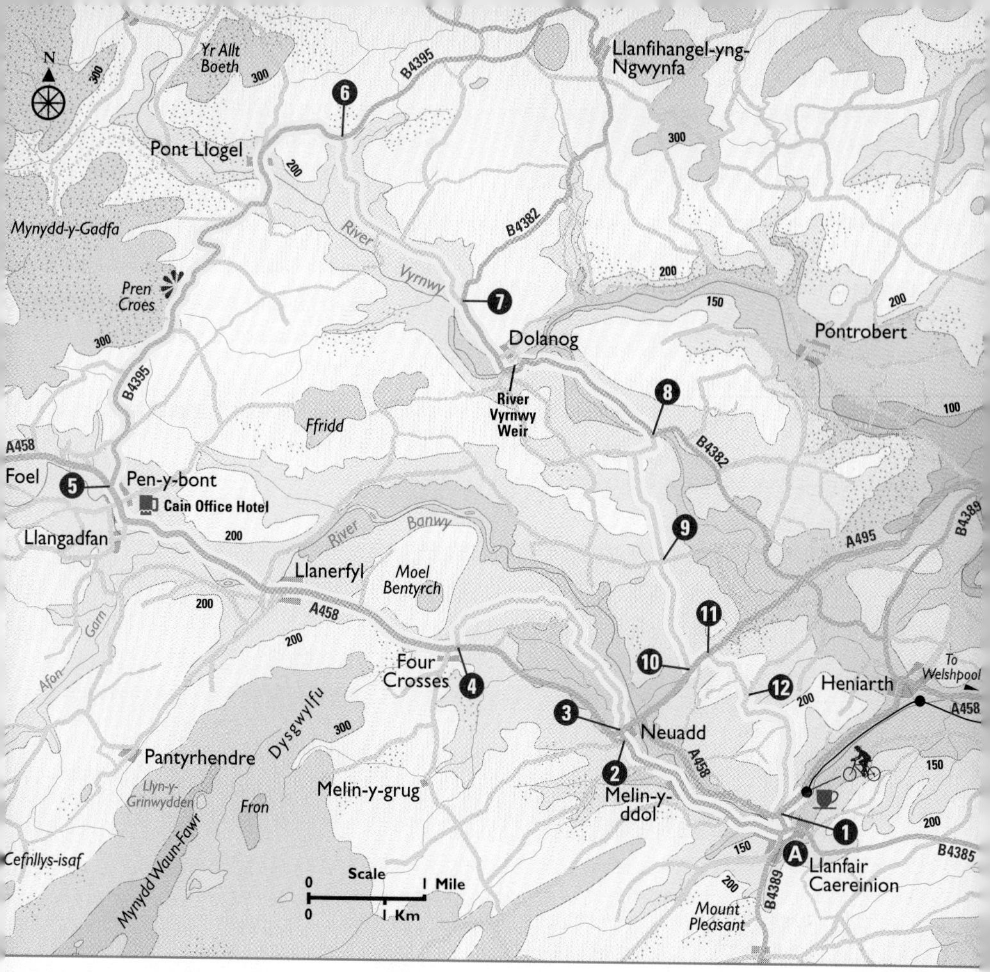

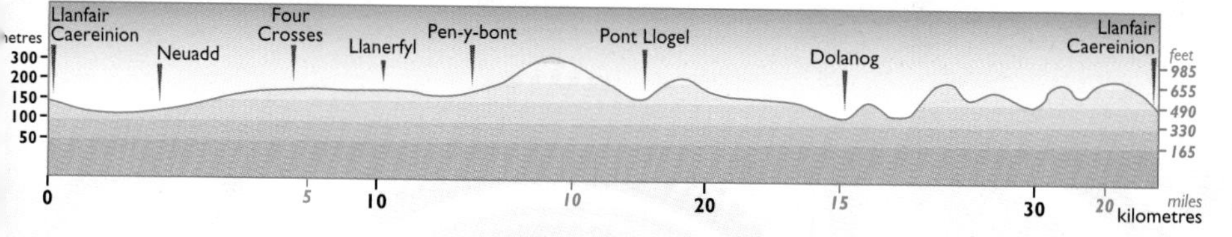

9 SO at XR, SP Llanfair Caereinion 3.

10 TL onto A495, no SP.

11 Take first TR and climb, no SP.

30.5km (19 miles)

12 Take first TR at unmarked junction and descend to Llanfair Caereinion, no SP. Then TL at TJ onto A458, no SP. Continue to station and the end of the route.

34km (21 miles)

Places of interest along the route

Ⓐ Llanfair Caereinion

The small town of Llanfair Caereinion was once a flannel-making centre. Today it is the main terminus of the Welshpool and Llanfair Railway. The narrow gauge railway was first opened in 1903 and carried passengers and goods until its closure in 1956. In 1963 the railway was purchased by the preservation society who have restored the railway along its full length. Steam trains run April to October and in December. Telephone (01938) 810441 for details.

Food and drink

There is a café at Llanfair Caereinion Station and there is plenty of choice in Welshpool.

Cain Office Hotel, Llangadfan
Meals available.

Rural Wales

Route
10

THE DYFI VALLEY – MACHYNLLETH AND COMMINS COCH

Route information

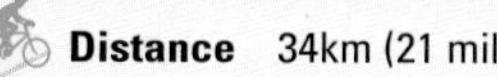

Distance 34km (21 miles)

Grade Strenuous

Terrain Ranging from valleys to rolling moorland, with several steep ascents and descents.

Time to allow 2 – 3 hours, plus whatever time you spend at the Centre for Alternative Technology.

Getting there by car Machynlleth is on the A489. The route starts in the public car park (pay and display) almost opposite the Tourist Information Centre in Newtown Road.

Getting there by train There is a railway station at Machynlleth. Telephone (0345) 484950 for information. Join the route as it passes the station entrance – TR out of station and continue to direction 2.

This route covers the hilly country around Machynlleth in the Dyfi Valley, and includes a short detour to the Centre for Alternative Technology. From here the route follows the railway line north east to Commins Coch before turning onto minor roads back to Machynlleth.

Places of interest along the route

A Machynlleth

The town is a popular holiday centre with an ornate clock tower in its centre. **Celtica** introduces visitors to the sights and sounds of Wales' Celtic past using the most up-to-date audio-visual technology. Tearoom and gift shop. Open all year, daily 1000–1800. Charge. Telephone (01654) 702702.

B Centre for Alternative Technology (CAT), near Machynlleth

North of Machynlleth, CAT comprises 3ha (7 acres) of environmental solutions – from a water powered cliff railway to organic gardens, and with wind, water and solar power displays. Café, picnic areas and gift shop. Open all year, daily from 1000 (July and August 0930); last entry 1730 (November to March 1600); site open until 1900 or dusk if earlier. Charge (but if you arrive by bicycle you get a 50% discount). Telephone (01654) 702400.

Food and drink

There are hotels and cafés in Machynlleth and a café at CAT. You might want to carry food and drink for the ride.

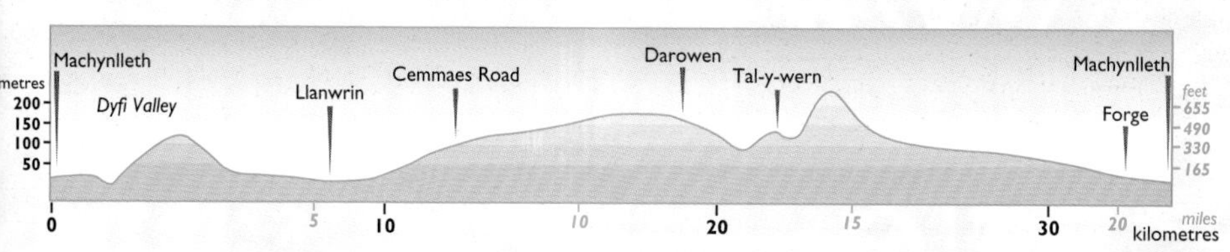

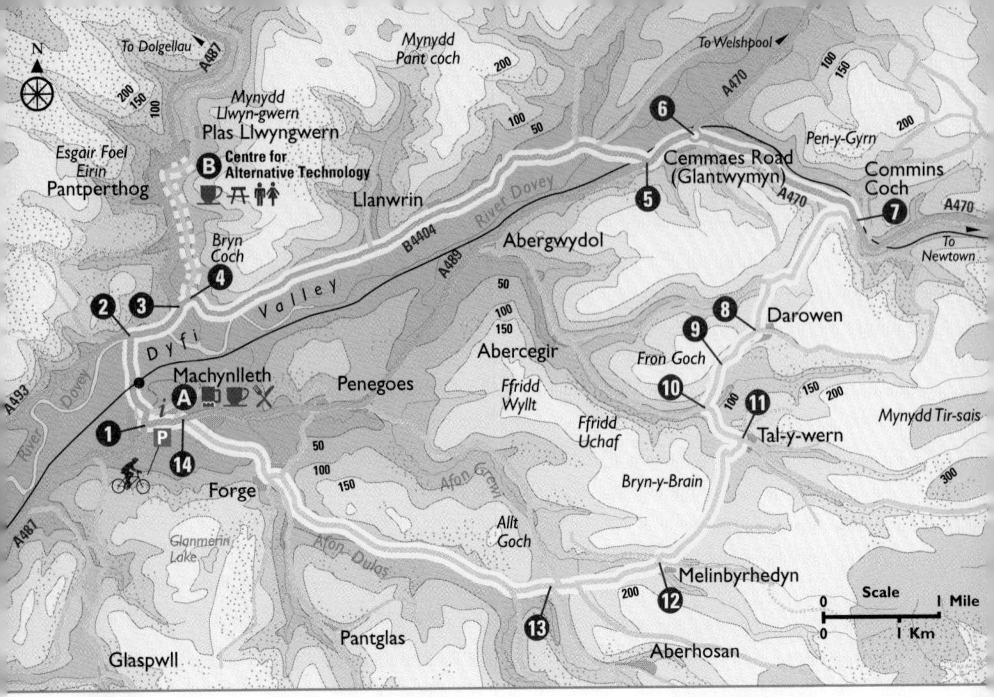

N
To Dolgellau A487
Mynydd Pant coch
To Welshpool
Mynydd Llwyn-gwern
Plas Llwyngwern
Esgair Foel Eirin
Pantperthog
B Centre for Alternative Technology
Llanwrin
Cemmaes Road (Glantwymyn)
A470
Pen-y-Gyrn
Commins Coch
To Newtown
River Dovey
B4404
A489
Abergwydol
Bryn Coch
Dyfi Valley
Darowen
Fron Goch
Abercegir
Machynlleth
A
Penegoes
Ffridd Wyllt
Ffridd Uchaf
Tal-y-wern
Mynydd Tir-sais
A493
A487
Forge
Afon Crewi
Bryn-y-Brain
Allt Goch
Glanmerin Lake
Afon Dulas
Melinbyrhedyn
Pantglas
Aberhosan
Glaspwll
Scale 0 1 Mile
0 1 Km

Route description

TL out of car park and head down main street towards the conspicuous clock tower.

1 TR, SP Dolgellau. Continue on this road, passing railway station.

2 TR at TJ onto A493, SP Dolgellau.

3 TR onto B4404, SP Llanwrin. Cross bridge.

4 To visit CAT TL after bridge, SP CAT, and ascend narrow lane to TR at TJ, SP CAT (5km/ 3 miles). After visit retrace route to bridge and TL onto B4404.

Otherwise continue along this road, crossing River Dovey.

5 TL at TJ onto A489, SP Welshpool.

15km (9.5 miles)

6 TR WITH CARE at roundabout, SP Newtown.

7 TR, SP Darowen, and climb steeply. Then bear right, no SP. Continue on this road into Darowen.

8 Keep R in Darowen, no SP.

9 Bear L down steep hill, no SP.

22km (13.5 miles)

10 TL at TJ, no SP.

11 TR, SP Melinbyrhedyn. Cross stream and climb.

12 TR over stream, SP Machynlleth, and climb. ***25.5km (16 miles)***

13 TR at TJ, SP Forge/Machynlleth. Take care on this steep descent.

14 TL at TJ into Newtown Road. Continue and TL into car park to complete the ride.

34km (21 miles)

If returning to the station, continue past car park, TR, SP Dolgellau, and return to station.

Route **11**

THE VALE OF CLWYD – ST ASAPH AND MAEN ACHWYFAEN

Route information

Distance 37km (23 miles)

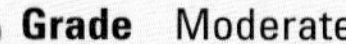

Grade Moderate

Terrain Tarmac roads throughout and two stretches of gated road forbidden to motorised traffic. The first 12km (7.5 miles) involves a climb of 200m (656 feet), but from here the road is more or less level until a final 6km (4 miles) downhill.

Time to allow 3–5 hours.

Getting there by car St Asaph is easily accessed from the A55, 48km (30 miles) west of Chester. Park in the car park by the River Elwy.

Getting there by train The nearest rail station is at Rhyl, 8km (5 miles) from St Asaph. Telephone (0345) 484950 for travel information. To join the route, TR out of station onto A526. Continue across A547 onto A5151 and follow road to just before Trelawnyd where TR to pass church on right, no SP. Continue route at direction 19.

From St Asaph the route follows the River Elwy for a climb through Tremeirchion. On along a bridleway for further climbing through Llanasa and Trelawnyd before dropping steeply back to St Asaph. During the first part of the ride there are splendid views over the Vale of Clwyd to Snowdonia, and over the Dee Estuary in the latter stages.

Route description

TR out of car park and cross bridge over river. TL at roundabout onto B5381.

1 TL to stay on B5381, SP Denbigh.

2 TL at TJ onto A525, SP St Asaph.

4km (2.5 miles)

3 TR, SP Tremeirchion.

4 TR at TJ, SP Bodfari. Then TL steeply uphill by memorial seat, SP Holywell. This is a splendid viewpoint westward over the Vale of Clwyd, with Snowdonia clearly visible in good weather.

5 TR at top of hill into wooded lane, no SP.

11km (7 miles)

6 TL at minor XR.

7 SO at XR, no SP.

8 TL at XR onto B5122, no SP.

14.5km (9 miles)

9 SO at XR.

10 TL into lane, SP No Through Road, and cross A55 via bridleway/cycleway bridge. Immediately after bridge continue as lane passes through farmyard via two gates.

11 TR at TJ, no SP.

12 SO WITH CARE at XR across A5151, SP Mostyn.

13 Keep L following SP Llanasa.

14 Keep L around field (containing Maen Achwyfaen). Then take RHF, no SP.

15 SO at XR, SP Llanasa (viewpoint here).

16 Keep L, passing Red Lion pub and church on RHS, SP Trelawnyd/Gwaenysgor.

24km (15 miles)

17 At end of village TL uphill, no SP. Continue to pass Gap Hill Tumulus on RHS.

18 TR onto A5151, SP Rhyl/Dyserth. If you started from Rhyl Station, continue on A5151 and retrace route to station. Otherwise, TL off A5151 to pass church on RHS, no SP.

19 TR at TJ by grass triangle, no SP.

29km (18 miles)

20 TL, SP Rhuallt.

21 TR, SP Cwm/Rhuallt. Then SO, SP Rhuallt.

22 Take RHF onto narrow lane for steep downhill, no SP. Then SO WITH CARE at XR, no SP.

River Dee

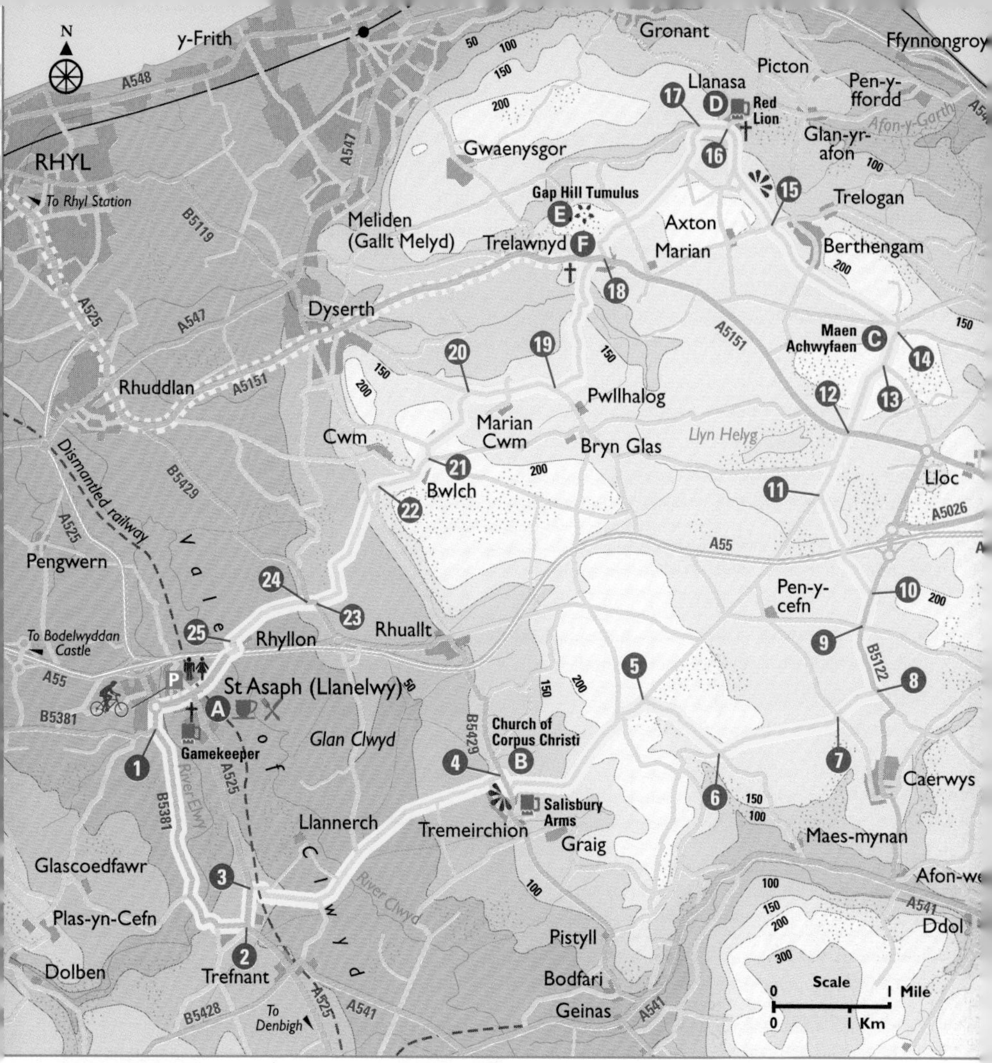

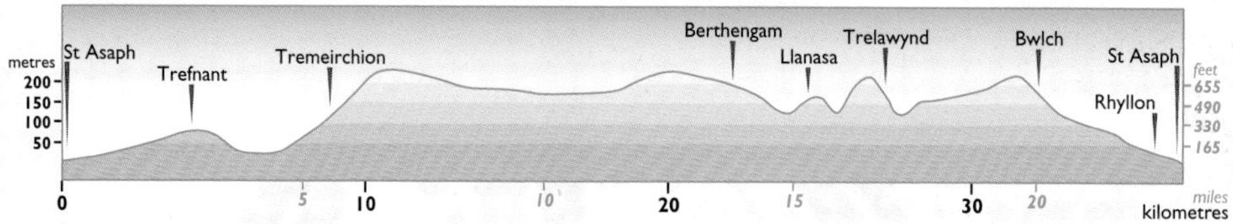

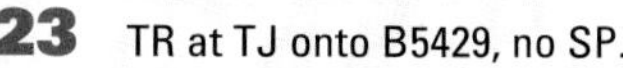

23 TR at TJ onto B5429, no SP.

24 TL into Lon Tai Cochion, SP No Through Road. ***34km (21 miles)***

25 TL through gate, SP Bridleway, and cross A55 via bridleway/cycleway bridge. After crossing bridge, TR uphill into St Asaph. Continue SO down High Street, passing Cathedral on LHS, and return to car park and the end of the route. ***37km (23 miles)***

Places of interest along the route

A St Asaph

St Asaph sits between the Rivers Clwyd and Elwy and is a city due to the its **cathedral**, one of the smallest in the country. There has been a religious building on the site of the cathedral since 560AD when a church was founded by St Icentigen. His successor, Asaph, gave his name to the city. The present cathedral building dates mainly from the 13th century and has many interesting features, both ancient and modern. The **parish church** is in perpendicular style and was restored in the late 1800s. Access to both the cathedral and parish church by donation. Telephone Rhyl Tourist Information Centre for further information on (01745) 355068. Just outside St Asaph, on the A55, is **Bodelwyddan Castle**, a restored Victorian country house containing a major collection of 19th-century portraits and photography on loan from the National Portrait Gallery in London. There is also furniture from the Victoria & Albert Museum and sculpture from the Royal Academy. Also magnificent grounds and gardens. Gift shop and tearoom. Open April to October, Saturday–Thursday 1100–1700; November to March, Tuesday–Thursday and weekends 1100–1600. Charge. Telephone (01745) 584060.

B Church of Corpus Christi, Tremeirchion

This is the only medieval church in the country dedicated in the name of Corpus Christi. The present bell was cast at Wigan in 1778. The church contains two fonts. The old 14th-century font was considered unsightly and was replaced (though not destroyed) in 1879. Access by donation. Contact Rhyl Tourist Information Centre for further information.

C Maen Achwyfaen

Also know as the Stone of Lamentation, this is Britain's tallest wheeled cross – 3.5m (12 feet) high and over 0.5m (2 feet) wide at its base. Maen Achwyfaen is unusual in that while the faces are covered with knotwork and chains typical of Viking sculpture, the sides depict animals associated with Celtic art. It is believed to date from the 10th century.

D Llanasa

Winner of the Best Kept Village award on several occasions, this is an attractive place with several ponds and an unusual rough stone steeple at the church.

E Gap Hill Tumulus, near Trelawnyd

To the right of the road just before reaching Trelawnyd, Gap Hill Tumulus is reputed to be the largest in Britain at 274m (900 feet) in circumference. The tumulus is said to be close to the site of a battle between the Iceni, led by Boadicea, and the Romans.

F Trelawnyd

In Trelawnyd churchyard, to the south of the church, stands a tall carved 12th-century cross. One side depicts the Crucifiction and the other St John.

Food and drink

Plenty of choice in St Asaph. Refreshments are also available at Bodelwyddan Castle.

Salisbury Arms, Tremeirchion
Meals served.

Red Lion, Llanasa
Food available.

Route 12

TYWYN AND TAL-Y-ILYN

Route information

Distance 40km (25 miles)

Grade Easy

Terrain Mostly along river valleys, with a few easy climbs. The roads are quiet except for a section of the A493, generally only moderately busy except for weekends at the height of the holiday season.

Time to allow 3 hours.

Getting there by car Tywyn is on the A493 and can be also reached from Dolgellau via the B4405. A one way traffic system operates in Tywyn – follow SP to free public car park.

Getting there by train There is a mainline railway station at Tywyn. Telephone (0345) 484950 for travel information. Exit station and follow SP to free public car park, the start of the ride.

From Tywyn north east along the Fathew valley to Abergynolwyn and onto to Tal-y-Ilyn, with an optional circuit of Tal-y-Ilyn lake. The return route follows the Dysynni valley back to Tywyn.

Places of interest along the route

A Tal-y-Ilyn Railway, Tywyn

The railway runs steam locomotives along a narrow gauge line. The line was opened in 1865 between Tywyn and Nant Gwernol. In 1950 the railway was saved from closure by the preservation society, whose members today provide the train crew and station staff. The **Narrow Gauge Railway Museum** displays locomotives, wagons, signals and many other interesting items. Refreshments are available at Tywyn and Abergynolwyn stations. Trains run February to October and during December. The museum is open when there are trains running. Telephone (01654) 710472 for further information. You could take a train from Tywyn to Abergynolwyn and follow the route from there.

Food and drink

There are two hotels in Tal-y-Ilyn and the narrow gauge railway stations at Tywyn and Abergynolwyn both have cafés.

Tearoom, near Trychiad

Passed towards the end of the ride.

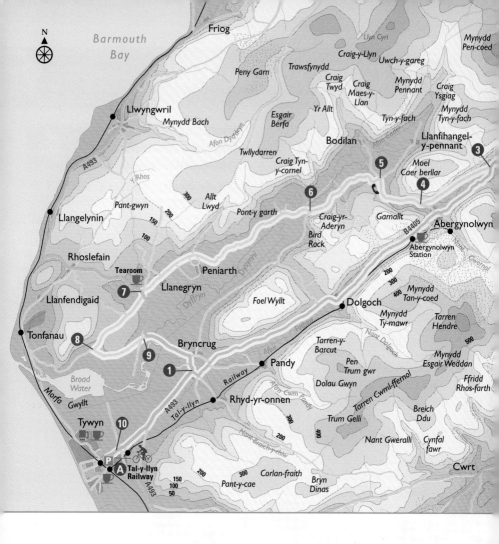

N
Barmouth Bay
Friog
Llyn Cyri
Mynydd Pen-coed
Craig-y-Llyn
Uwch-y-gareg
Peny Garn
Trawsfynydd
Craig Twyd
Craig Maes-y-Llan
Mynydd Pennant
Craig Ysgiag
Llwyngwril
Mynydd Bach
Esgair Berfa
Yr Allt
Tyn-y-fach
Mynydd Tyn-y-fach
Afon Dyffryn
Bodilan
Afon Cader
Llanfihangel-y-pennant
3
A493
Twllydarren
Craig Tyn-y-cornel
5
Moel Caer berllar
Y Rhos
4
300
Allt Lwyd
6
Pant-gwyn
200
Pont-y garth
Craig-yr-Aderyn
Gamallt
Llangelynin
150
B4405
Abergynolwyn
100
Bird Rock
Abergynolwyn Station
Rhoslefain
Nant Gwernol
Tearoom
Peniarth
Dysynni
200
300
7
Llanegryn
Mynydd Tan-y-coed
400
Llanfendigaid
Dyffryn
Foel Wyllt
Dolgoch
Mynydd Ty-mawr
Tarren Hendre
Fathew
Tonfanau
8
Nant Dolgoch
500
Tarren-y-Barcut
9
Bryncrug
Afon
Mynydd Esgair Weddan
Pandy
Pen Trum gwr
1
Broad Water
Railway
Ffridd Rhos-farth
Tarren Cwml-ffernol
Dolau Gwyn
Afon Cwm Pandy
Morfa Gwyllt
Rhyd-yr-onnen
Tal-y-llyn
A493
Breich Ddu
300
Trum Gelli
Tywyn
10
Nant Breich-y-rhiw
200
400
Nant Gweralli
Cynfal fawr
P
A
Tal-y-llyn Railway
Cwrt
200
300
Corlan-fraith
150
100
50
Pant-y-cae
Bryn Dinas
A493

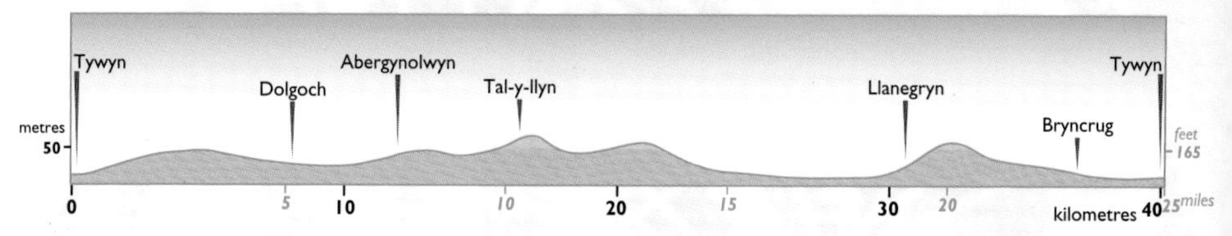
Tywyn
Dolgoch
Abergynolwyn
Tal-y-llyn
Llanegryn
Bryncrug
Tywyn
metres
50
feet
165
0
5
10
10
20
15
30
20
kilometres 40
25 miles

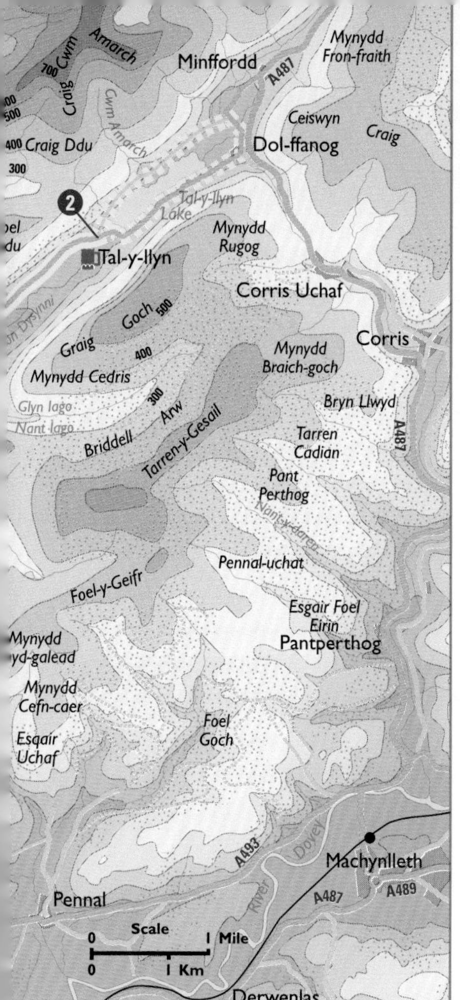

Route description 

TL out of car park and immediately TL again, following one way SP. Almost immediately TR by Barclays Bank, no SP. Keep in left lane and continue out of town, passing Corbett Arms Hotel on LHS.

1 TR onto B4405, SP Tal-y-llyn (3km/2 miles). Follow road as it climbs gently up valley with superb views of the mountains ahead of you. Continue through Abergynolwyn to Tal-y-llyn. (If using the train as far as Abergynolwyn, TR out of station onto B4405 and continue to Tal-y-llyn.)

2 Arrive Tal-y-llyn. To circuit the lake, TL and ride all the way around making a TR at the far end (an extra 5.5km/3.5 miles).

To continue, retrace route down hill for approximately 1.5km (1 mile) and:

3 TR, SP Llanegryn. ***19km (12 miles)***

4 TR at TJ, SP Llanfihangel.

5 Keep L by telephone box, SP Bryncrug.

6 Keep R, SP Llanegryn (25km/15.5 miles). The prominent crag on LHS is Bird Rock. Continue, passing tearoom on RHS.

7 TL, SP Tywyn, and immediately TR, no SP.

8 TL at TJ, no SP. ***33km (20.5 miles)***

9 TR at TJ, no SP. Almost immediately TR at TJ onto A493, no SP. Continue on A493 into Tywyn.

10 TL off one way system into car park or return to mainline station.

40km (25 miles)

Route **13**

PANORAMA ROAD AND WORLD'S END

Route information

Distance 43km (27 miles)

Grade Strenuous

Terrain Mostly minor roads passing through small villages and open countryside. Hilly in places, but with magnificent views. Watch out for stray sheep!

Time to allow 3–4 hours.

Getting there by car Moss Valley Park is signposted from the B5433, 2km (1 mile) from Wrexham. There is ample free car parking.

Getting there by train Moss Valley Park is 4km (2.5 miles) from Wrexham mainline station. Telephone (0345) 484950 for travel information. TR out of station and TL at roundabout. SO at next roundabout, under flyover, and take first TR onto B5433. Moss Valley is signposted 2km (1 mile) on RHS.

From the beautifully landscaped Moss Valley Park, the route passes through the outskirts of Wrexham to the village of Bersham and then climbs to the Welsh mining village of Penycae. On for more climbing up to the Panorama Road with magnificent views high above the Vale of Llangollen. Passing the ancient fortress of Dinas Bran, the route turns to follow Eglwyseg Mountain through to World's End and then over the Esclusham moorland. A descent to Minera leads to one final climb to Coedpoeth. The route then runs downhill most of the way back to Moss Valley Park.

Food and drink

The middle section of the route is remote and the tea stops are only open in summer. Carry a supply of food and drink to sustain you during the ride – there are many ideal picnic spots along the route.

Prospect Farm Tearoom, Garth
Light teas, home made food and beautiful views.

Eglwyseg Tearoom, near World's End
Light teas offered at this attractive spot by a stream.

City Arms, Minera
Pub with restaurant offering a good choice of food. Open all year.

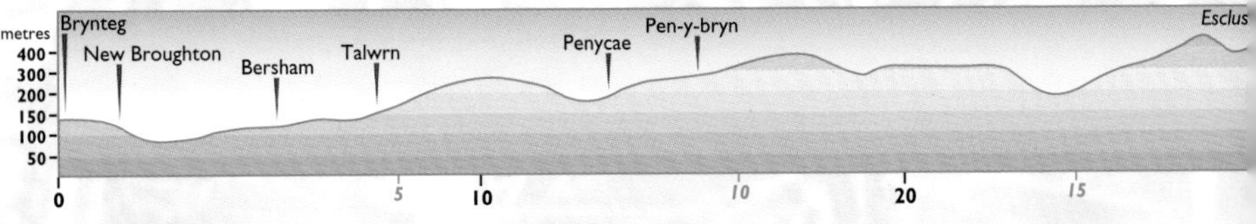

Places of interest along the route

A Moss Valley Park
This area was once disfigured by industrial dereliction but has been transformed into a leisure park offering walking, fishing, horse riding and golf. Free access at all reasonable times (charge for activities). Telephone Wrexham County Borough Council for further information on (01978) (385916).

B Bersham Ironworks and Heritage Centre
The centre describes the story of John 'Iron Mad' Wilkinson and his famous 18th-century ironworks which produced cannons for the American War of Independence and cylinders for James Watt's steam engines. Heritage Centre (admission free) open all year; ironworks (charge) open Easter to September. Telephone (01978) 261529 for further information.

C Castell Dinas Bran
The ruins of an ancient castle (known locally as Crow Castle) set high on a hill overlooking the Vale of Llangollen. Free access at all reasonable times.

D Minera Lead Mines, near Wrexham
At the head of the Clywedog Valley, Minera comprises a country park and the remains of the lead mines. The working museum illustrates how lead was mined in the 19th-century and how the area has been mined since Roman times for lead, coal, limestone and silica. Country park open at all reasonable times. Telephone for details of museum opening on (01978) 762122.

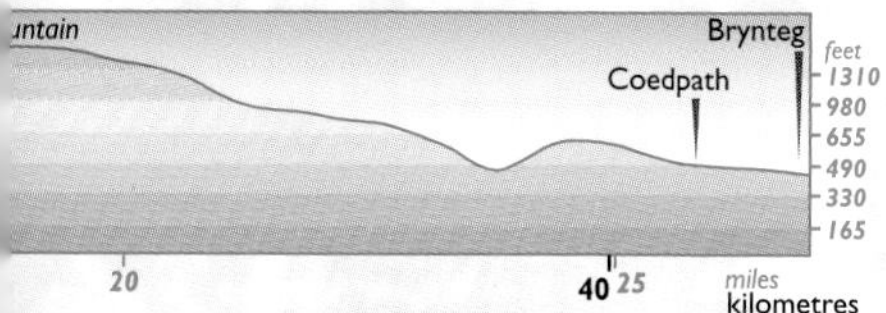

E Nant Mill Visitor Centre, near Wrexham
Housed in this former corn mill are exhibitions offering an insight into the life of the Clywedog Valley, including a giant mole tunnel. Picnic area. Open Easter to September, Tuesday–Sunday 1000–1630; October to Easter, weekends only. Telephone (j01978) 752772.

Route description

Start from the larger of the two car parks (the one with the childrens' playground) at the Moss Valley Park. TL and climb hill, under railway bridge. TL onto B5433, SP Wrexham.

1 TL at junction, SP Wrexham. Pass under flyover then TR at roundabout, SP Technology Park. TR at next roundabout, SP Ruthin.

2 TR onto A525, SP Ruthin. Take next TL into Berse Lane (B5098), SP Bersham, and continue alongside Wrexham bypass.

3 TR at TJ, SP Nant Mill. Bersham Heritage Centre is dead ahead (5.5km/3.5 miles). Keep L on bend to TR onto B5097 and continue past water tower.

4 TL into lane (after water tower), no SP. Continue to follow lane for 2.5km (1.5 miles).

5 TL at TJ by farm. Take next TR (opposite Onen Fawr farm entrance). Continue into Penycae.

6 TR in Penycae, uphill into Hill Street. Then TR at TJ (by War Memorial) into Chapel Lane, SP Pen-y-bryn.

7 TR at TJ, SP Prospect Farm Tearoom (17km/10.5 miles). Pass tearoom.

8 SO at junction (past Prospect Farm), over cattle grid and onto Panorama Road. Continue, passing Castell Dinas Bran. In the valley you

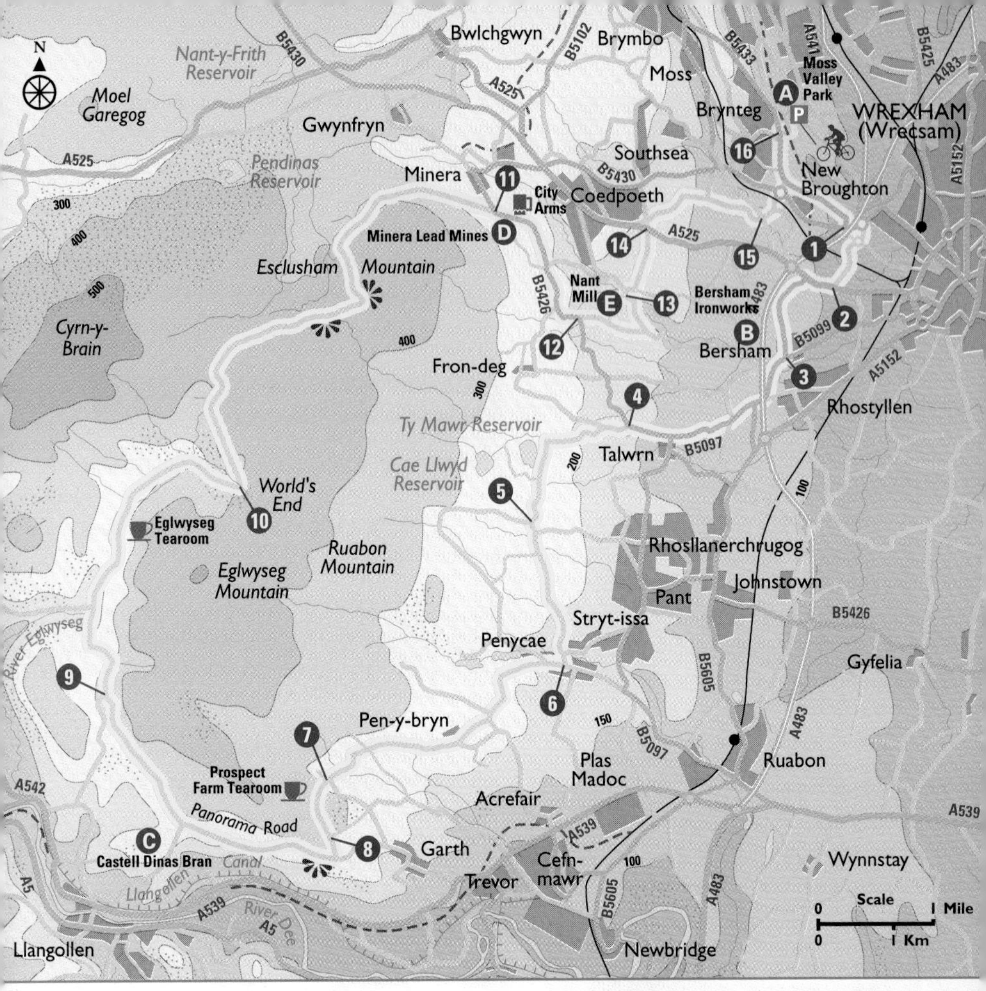

will see the River Dee, the Llangollen Canal, the A5 and the steam railway.

9 TR at TJ, SP World's End.
22.5km (14 miles)

10 Arrive World's End. The cliff on RHS is Eglwyseg Mountain. Take care at ford as you climb up to open moors. Continue for long descent with views over Wrexham and Cheshire.

11 TR at TJ, no SP. Pass Minera Lead Mine Museum. ***33.5km (21 miles)***

12 TL on bend, SP Bersham, for 1km (0.6 mile). Take second TL, SP Nant Mill. Cross Nant Bridge and climb past Nant Mill Visitor Centre.
37.5km (23.5 miles)

13 TR at TJ, SP Coedpoeth.

14 Cross A535 WITH CARE into Heol Offa. Take first TR at XR and descend for 1.5km (1 mile).

15 Cross main road into Bersham Road (41.5km/26 miles). Continue SO at roundabout, SP Pentre Broughton. Then TL onto B5433, SP Moss Valley Park.

16 TR downhill, SP Moss Valley Park. Pass under rail bridge and TR into Moss Valley car park to complete the ride. ***43km (27 miles)***

Route 14

RUTHIN AND THE CLOCLAENOG FOREST

Route information

Distance 53km (33 miles)

Grade Strenuous

Terrain Mainly quiet undulating lanes and B roads, with one off-road section along a firm track (suitable for a touring bike although it can be bypassed on tarmac roads if desired).

Time to allow 3–6 hours.

Getting there by car Ruthin is in the Vale of Clwyd at the junction of the A494 and A525. Park at the Castle car park.

Getting there by train There is no practical rail access to this ride.

From Ruthin for a steady climb to the Clocaenog Forest. Initially following the Afon Clwyedog, the route reaches a height of 400m (1312.5 feet) before descending to Llyn Brenig. From there the route climbs again, offering excellent views of the Berwyns and Snowdonia. A descent to Cerrigydrudion is followed by a further climb back to the Clocaenog Forest for a long descent to Ruthin.

Places of interest along the route

A Ruthin

An interesting historic town with many fine buildings, including the 16th-century Nantclwyd Hall just off St Peter's Square, and the Old Court House built in 1401. Ruthin Craft Centre comprises ten workshops displaying a range of crafts, a café and the Tourist Information Centre (telephone 01824 703992).

B Clocaenog Forest and Llyn Brenig

A working forest providing soft wood for a range of industries and an important wildlife habitat. Situated in the forest is **Llyn Brenig**, a

Ruthin

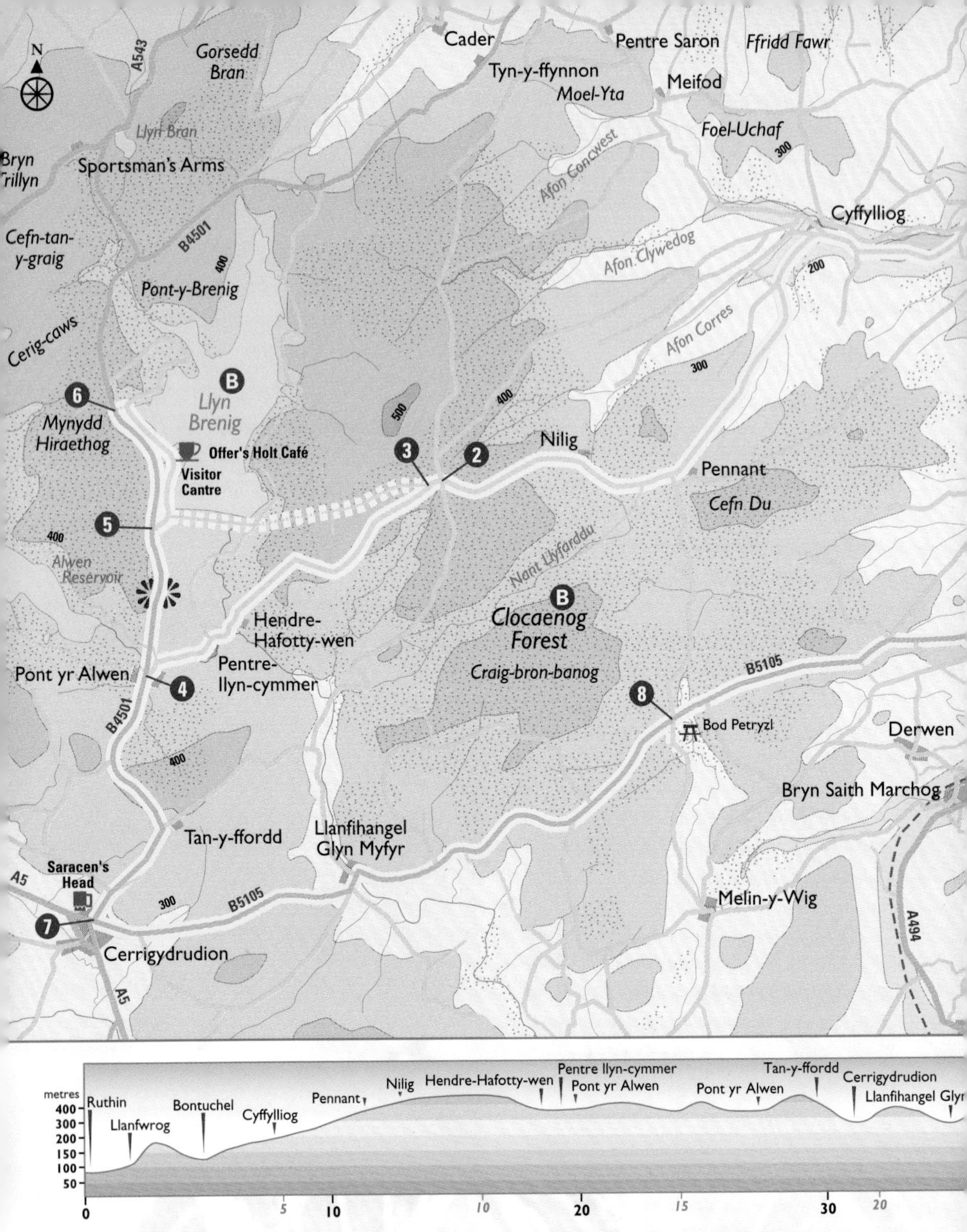

man-made lake which is used in conjunction with Llyn Tegid and Llyn Celyn to control the flow of the River Dee (which used to be prone to severe and frequent flooding in its lower reaches above Chester). The lake creates a useful wildlife habitat and provides opportunities for watersports, fishing and walking. There is a cycle trail around the lake and nature reserve. The visitor centre has exhibitions, café and shop. Bicycles can be hired. Free access to forest/lake at all reasonable times. Visitor centre open Easter to October, daily 1000–1700. Telephone Ruthin Tourist Information Centre for further information.

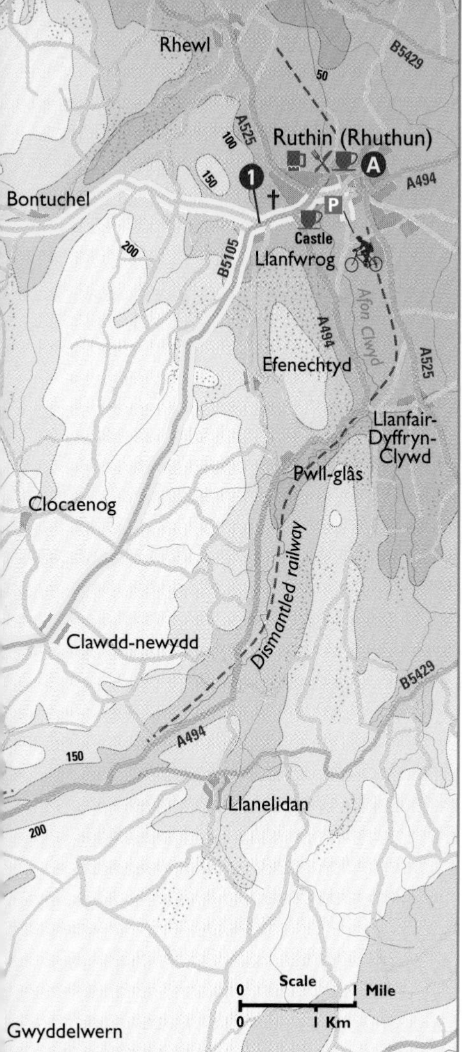

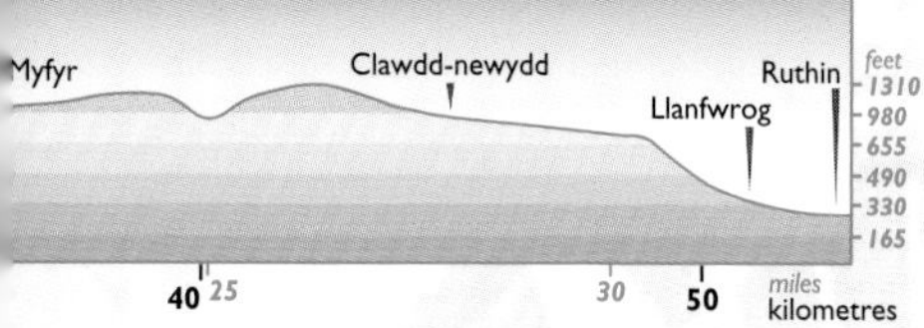

Route description

TL out of Castle car park and then TL at TJ onto A494, SP Bala. Continue (as road becomes B5105) into Llanfwrog (do NOT follow A494 L), pass church on RHS and descend.

1 TR, SP Bontuchel/Cyffylliog. Cycle through Bontuchel, Cyffylliog and Pennant and continue to XR.

2 SO at XR, no SP. ***14km (8.5 miles)***

3 To continue on-road bear L and follow SP to Pentre-llyn-Cwmer. Climb and descend through village to TJ with B4501 and continue at direction 4.

For the off-road option, TR, no SP. Climb past Isgaerwen Farm onto track and continue to cattle grid (by lake) where bear L and follow track over dam. Bear R and continue route from direction 5.

4 TR, SP Llyn Brenig. ***19.5km (12 miles)***

5 TR, SP Llyn Brenig Visitor Centre, and follow SP to centre. After visit follow exit SP and bear L, SP Main Exit.

6 TL at TJ onto B4501, no SP (23km/ 14.5 miles). Continue along B4501 for climb and descent to Cerrigydrudion.

7 TL at TJ onto B5105, SP Ruthin 14 (30.5km/19 miles). Continue on this road to XR.

8 To visit Bod Petryal picnic site, TR. Otherwise, continue on B5105. Cycle through Clawdd-newydd and descend to Ruthin, retracing route to Castle car park and the end of the ride. ***53km (33 miles)***

Food and drink

Ruthin has plenty of tearooms and pubs, including the Castle Car Park Café, CTC listed and a popular cyclist's stop (closed Tuesdays). There is a picnic site at Bod Petryal and refreshments are available at Llyn Brenig visitor centre.

Saracen's Head, Cerrigydrudion
Serves meals and bar snacks.

Route 15

CHESTER, HOPE MOUNTAIN AND HANDBRIDGE

Route information

Distance 54.5km (34 miles)

Grade Moderate

Terrain Flat roads and evenly graded climbs. Some of the hills up to the top of Hope Mountain are steep but can be walked if your bicycle's gears are not low enough. Suitable for moderately fit cyclists.

Time to allow 4–8 hours.

Getting there by car Chester is well served by motorways and trunk roads. The route starts from the railway station (signposted from the central ring road, but best approached from the north).
There are short- and long-term car parks close to the railway station – choose with care as prices vary considerably.

Getting there by train Chester is on the main line between Crewe and Holyhead and has good connections to Liverpool, Manchester and beyond. However, most trains from Crewe are Sprinters with restricted cycle capacity. Telephone (0345) 484950 for travel information.

This route starts in historic Chester, surrounded by its red sandstone Roman and medieval walls and the River Dee. The route climbs gently into Wales, dropping briefly into the Alyn valley at Hope before the climb up Hope Mountain for spectacular vistas across the Cheshire Plain and on further into Wales. The return is a gentle descent along quiet lanes eventually approaching Chester from the south. The start of the route avoids the traffic and goes through some less well explored areas of Chester via stretches of canal towpath (you must have a permit to cycle along the towpath – see page 8). An alternative on-road route is given.

Route description

To use the canal towpath, leave the station and head SO at roundabout along City Road for 300m. Cross canal bridge, dismount, descend steps on LHS to canal towpath. TL under City Road and follow towpath (or accompanying road when available). Arrive Fortress pub, pass under road bridge into deep rock cutting. (Eastgate crosses almost 30.5m/100 feet above you next to the infamous Bridge of Sighs from which condemned prisoners threw themselves). Pass ancient water tower on LHS and continue under inner ring road bridge. Pass locks, go under railway bridge and take LHF on track to emerge by Telford's Warehouse. At end of track, TR for 5m, remount, then immediately TL, away from Telford's Warehouse, to descend to Sealand Road. TR, no SP, passing through traffic lights.

River Dee, Chester

DEVA

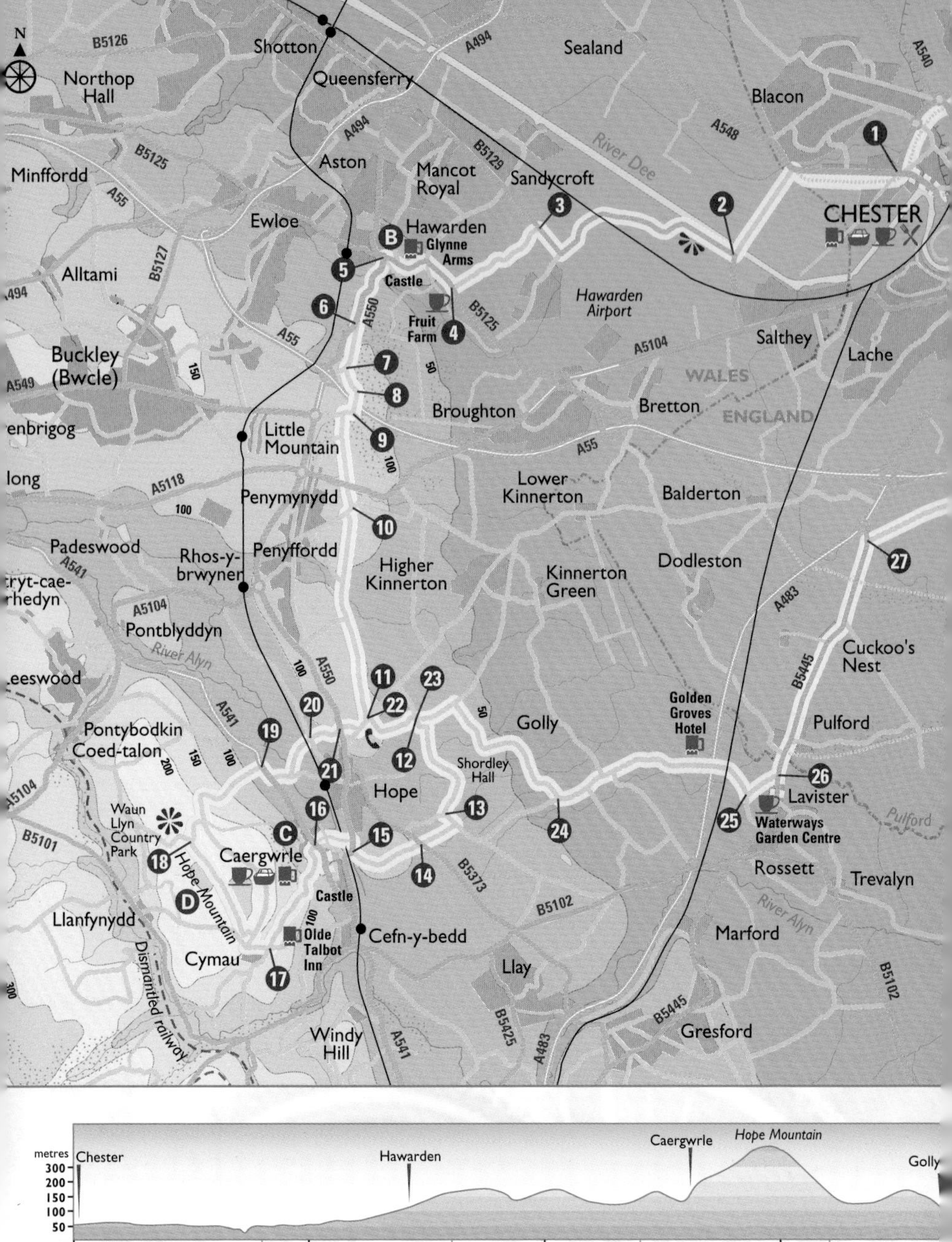

To stay on-road, leave station and TR at roundabout into Station Road. SO at traffic lights (by Railway Inn). Keep L on St Anns Street. TR by fire station onto cycle path. At the end of the path, dismount, cross junction, TR along Victoria Road (sports centre and car park RHS). Continue over railway bridge, TL at TJ. Then TR at mini roundabout. SO over next mini roundabout. TL at roundabout (by Safeway) into Countess Way, SP Blacon/Sealand Road (there

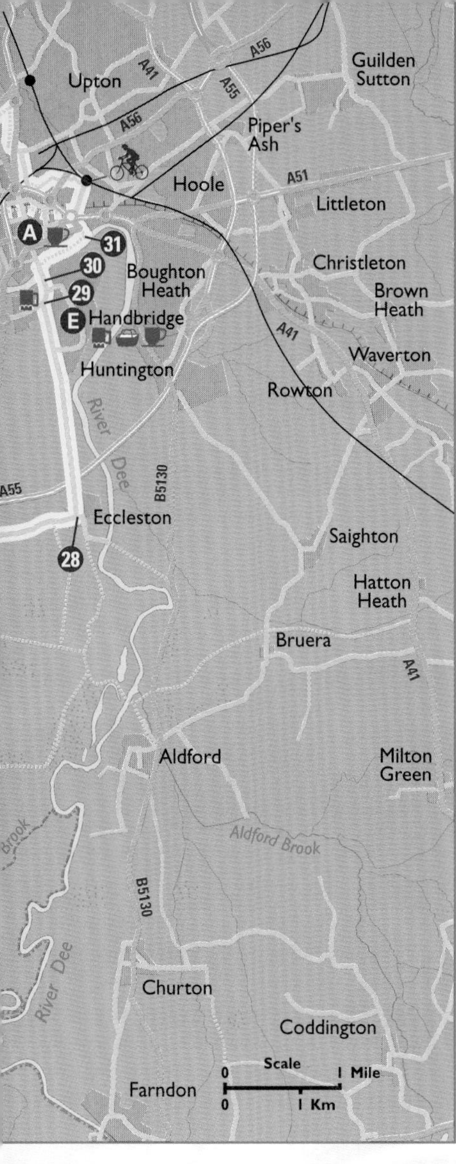

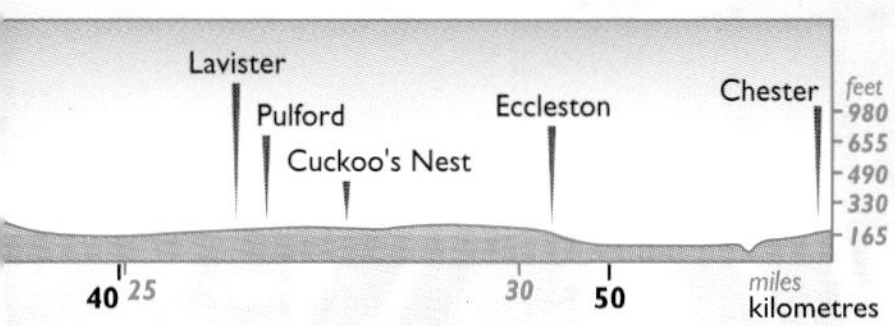

is a cycle path here. Take second exit at next roundabout (by Newgate Motors), SP A5480/ Queensferry. Pass under two bridges. SO at XR, SP A5480/Queensferry. SO at roundabout (by McDonalds), no sp. TR at XR (by Halfords).

1 Continue along Sealand Road (Retail Park on RHS). SO through two sets of traffic lights (cycle path on LHS may be used but be prepared for dismounting at many junctions). The cycle path ends (just after Park & Ride exit) – TL into Ferry Lane, SP No Through Road. Dismount at footbridge and cross over River Dee – you are now in Wales!

6.5km (4 miles)

2 TR into Flint Road. (At railway bridge, Russian Mig fighter planes can be seen on private airfield below together with views of Hawarden Castle and Hope Mountain.) Follow road round sharp right hand bend (SP Industrial Park) and:

3 TL into Rake Lane, no SP. Continue as lane begins to rise, passing through farmyard buildings. ***10.5km (6.5 miles)***

4 TR at TJ opposite entrance to Hawarden Fruit Farm. Follow this road into Hawarden village, passing stone cottages on LHS.

5 TL at XR by ornate fountain, SP Wrexham/ A550, for brief descent then climb. Pass small SP Lay-by and immediately:

6 TL into steep lane which runs alongside stone wall of wooded castle grounds.

7 LHF, SP No Through Road, following wall on LHS.

8 At end of lane continue through wooden barriers on LHS. The next turn is easy to miss – descend for approximately 300m and TR over footbridge. ***14km (8.5 miles)***

9 TR at TJ, then shortly TL at XR (by SP Footpath) into Old Hope Road. Pass radio transmitter on RHS. SO at XR, continuing on Old Hope Road. ***15.5km (9.5 miles)***

10 TR at staggered XR, then immediately TL into Lower Mountain Road.

11 SO at XR (by Estyn Lodge, telephone box opposite), SP Shordley. ***21.5km (13.5 miles)***

12 TR at XR, SP Shordley, and pass Shordley Hall.

13 Take LHF for 300m (grassy triangle in road), no SP. TR at TJ, no SP but Hope Mountain on RHS. ***24.5km (15 miles)***

14 SO at XR across B5373 onto Rhyddyn Hill, no SP.

15 TR at TJ by Bridge End Mews for 100m. TL into Fellows Lane, SP No Through road. Cross railway bridge, descend and cross pack-horse bridge over River Alyn for sharp rise. SO at XR, SP 2½ tonne weight limit. Continue onto main street in Caergwrle. ***26.5km (16.5 miles)***

16 To see Caergwrle Castle TL (entrance by war memorial, on LHS after Post Office).

Otherwise, continue SO at XR for 50m into Bryn Yorkin (car park on LHS). TL at XR. TR at TJ into Bryn Yorkin Lane. Start severe climb, keeping R at start and L by large stone gateway. Glimpses of Caergwrle Castle can be seen on LHS. ***28km (17.5 miles)***

17 TR at TJ by Olde Talbot Inn in Cymau. Immediately TR (by bench), SP appears to have been swung round so ignore. Continue on road for climb past farm. At hairpin bend take sharp TR (by SP Footpath). Then take LHS, SP Unsuitable for Heavy Vehicles, making for next hairpin bend by stone cottage. Follow RHS hairpin, complete long climb to top and descend briefly.

18 For a rest and breathtaking views, TL at TJ and TR over cattle grid into Waun-y-Llyn Country Park car park. Continue to end of gravel parking area and a short footpath leads to toposcope and views across Cheshire Plain. Retrace to cattle grid and TL (30.5km/19 miles).

Otherwise, continue for sharp descent towards Chester.

19 TR at TJ onto dual carriageway. Shortly after road narrows, TL into Fagl Lane, SP Sports Centre/Wrexham. Pass quarry entrance and TL into Pigeon House Lane. Cross railway.

20 SO at XR, continuing along Pigeon House Lane. ***34km (21 miles)***

21 SO at XR over A550 into Rhos Estyn Lane. TL at TJ, no SP.

22 TR by telephone box, SP Shordley.

23 SO at XR. TR at bottom of shallow dip, no SP but by telegraph pole. Continue past Oak Tree Farm and through Golly. ***39km (24 miles)***

24 TL at TJ, SP Burton Green. Pass Golden Groves Hotel, cross bridge over main road and level crossing.

25 TL, SP Pulford/Chester.

26 To visit Waterways Garden Centre, TR at TJ. Otherwise, TL onto B5445. Continue through Pulford, crossing Welsh/English border once more. Continue to shortly before roundabout with busy A483.

27 TR (before roundabout), SP Eccleston. Pass under bridge, through cutting and into Eccleston. ***46.5km (29 miles)***

28 TL, SP Chester (52km/32.5 miles). Continue into Handbridge.

29 TR at TJ opposite White Horse pub. Descend to River Dee.

30 Cross Old Dee Bridge. Dismount and pass under stone gateway (part of city walls), cross road and wheel bike through short pedestrianised area running alongside river. Remount and follow riverside path, carefully avoiding many pedestrians. SO at roundabout, through barriers and under suspension bridge, along The Groves.

31 Follow road away from river (stone wall of Grosvenor Park on LHS) and eventually arrive at busy Boughton dual carriageway (Amsterdam pub directly opposite). Dismount, cross dual carriageway WITH CARE (it is illegal to ride across this junction). Remount and briefly TR then TL (with fast food shop on corner). Dismount at TJ (by Harkers Pub – excellent beers). Climb steps on LHS to exit onto City Road. Cross road and continue to TR into station and complete the ride. ***54.5km (34 miles)***

Places of interest along the route

A Chester

There is a much to see in this Roman city, best toured on foot. There are a large number of old and fascinating buildings throughout Chester. Visitors can walk right around the city on the old city wall, over the old gates and past the defensive turrets. **Deva Roman Experience**, Bridge Street, is a reconstruction of Roman Chester. Tearoom and shop. Open all year, daily 0900–1700. Charge. Telephone (01244) 343407. **Chester Cathedral**, Northgate Street, is a magnificent building of dark red stone on the site of a 10th-century minster. In 1742 Handel gave his first public performance of *The Messiah* here. A copy of his marked score is on display. Open daily. Charge. The **Shropshire Union Canal** runs almost through the centre of Chester, connecting with the River Dee and leading into the Manchester Ship Canal. Various canal and river trips are on offer. For information on the many attractions in Chester, telephone the Tourist Information Centre on (01244) 402111.

B Hawarden

Mentioned in the Domesday Book, Hawarden has two castles – one a 13th-century ruin and the other once home of William Gladstone, the Victorian Prime Minster. In the picturesque grounds of the castle is the Black Sheep Gallery, displaying traditional and contemporary fine art. Tearoom. Open all year, Tuesday–Friday 1000–1800; weekends 1000–1700. Admission free. Telephone (01244) 535505.

C Caergwrle

On the site of a Bronze Age hillfort and a Roman station, the castle was built by Dafydd, brother of llewelyn the Last. The last rebellion against Edward I was launched from the castle in 1282. Free access at all reasonable times.

D Hope Mountain

Not technically a mountain at 281m (924 feet) but on a clear day you can see Blackpool Tower 78.5km (49 miles) away as well as Snowdon peak to the west, 68km (42 miles) distant. Try hard and you can almost see the station in Chester!

E Handbridge

Once a salmon fishing village, now a quietish backwater of Chester, joined to the city by the magnificent Old Dee Bridge. The waterside area, known as The Groves, is a picturesque and thronging place when the sunshines and at weekends.

Food and drink

Chester is well-served by cafés, restaurants and shops, open all year, at all times of day and night. The railway station has a buffet and the adjacent streets have pubs and cafés, as well as the usual fast food outlets. There are pubs, cafés and shops in Ceargwrle and Handbridge and ice creams and drinks can be bought at The Groves, towards the end of the ride.

Fruit Farm, Hawarden Castle
Soft drinks and fresh soft fruit in season.

Glynne Arms, Hawarden
Serves snacks and drinks.

Golden Groves, near Rossett
Open daily (except Mondays) for drinks, bar snacks and full meals. Outside seating.

Waterways Garden Centre, Lavister
The centre has a fine café, open daily.

Route 16

LLANSILIN AND LAKE VYRNWY

Route information

Distance 59.5km (37 miles)

Grade Strenuous

Terrain Hilly ground with some steep climbs and descents. One of the roads, classified as tarmac, is more like an off-road track, but it is down hill and rideable if taken steadily.

Time to allow 5–6 hours.

Getting there by car From Oswestry take the B4580 and follow this road for 10.5km (6.5 miles) to Llansilin. Continue SO through centre of village to car park on LHS, the start of the ride.

Getting there by train There is no practical railway access to this ride.

This area has been described by more than one person as 'God's own country'; it is not an original remark, but is very apt since the hills and valleys, and their many rivers and streams, provide superb scenery without any of man's so called improvements to spoil the effect. The lanes are narrow, often sunk between high hedges, which provide some shelter if the wind is blowing. There is little flat ground, the hills are often steep, both up and down, and the roads are invariably twisty. There are three climbs, each around 4.5km (3 miles) long. The road surfaces are generally good but you will encounter some poor sections as well as a covering of sand and soil after a period of heavy rain. The other bar to steady progress is the occasional stray sheep.

Places of interest along the route

A Lake Vyrnwy, near Dolanog

The lake is a man made reservoir constructed at the end of the last century to supply water to Liverpool. Due to its position amongst the surrounding hills, the dam itself is very unobtrusive and it comes as quite a surprise when you round the last bend in the road. On the dam

Food and drink

In view of the hilly nature of this ride you should carry an energy bar or two and plenty of drink. There are several pubs in Llanfyllin where you may get food and drink, depending on the time you pass through, and there is a café at Lake Vyrnwy.

Lake Vyrnwy Hotel, Lake Vyrnwy

Offering meals and superb views across the lake (but requires a short detour).

Wynnstay Inn, Llansilin

Next to the car park. Offering B&B as well as bar food and pots of tea. The opening hours vary with the time of year but the landlord is willing to open out of hours if you contact him in advance (01691 791355)

walls, either side of the road, are photographs and explanations of the area as the dam was being constructed. See route 9 for further details.

B Motte and Bailey

This is the site of an old motte and bailey castle. All that remains are the moat and the mound on which the structure was erected. Growing on the mound today is a magnificent oak tree and the short walk (100m) is worth the effort. Free access at all reasonable times.

Route description

TR out of car park, no SP.

1 TL, SP Moelfre, and climb.

2 TR by letter box, SP Moelfre.

3 TL, SP Efail Rhyd. Cross bridge and immediately TR, no SP. Follow road alongside lake road surface is not good for 3–5km (2–3 miles).

4 TL, SP Efail Rhyd. ***6.5km (4 miles)***

5 TR at TJ, no SP. ***7.5km (4.5 miles)***

6 TL, SP Pentrefelin.

7 TR, SP Llanrhaeadr.

8 TR at TJ onto B4580, SP Bala (11km/ miles). Soon bear L onto B4396, no SP.

9 Easy to miss – TL and climb, no SP. This is the start of a 5km (3 mile) climb so take it easy nd do not miss the wonderful views.

10 TL at TJ (by embankment wall on RHS), no SP.

11 SO up hill, by old Chapel on RHS (the main road bends sharply L).

12 RHF, continuing uphill.

13 Go through gateway across road and shortly reach top of this long climb (19km/ 12 miles). The surface deteriorates rapidly now so TAKE CARE!

14 TL at TJ, no SP.

15 TR at TJ, SP Lake Vyrnwy.

16 To visit Lake Vyrnwy Hotel continue SO for 1km (0.6 mile) and TR sharply uphill. After visit retrace route and cross dam.

Otherwise, TL across dam. ***25.5km (16 miles)***

17 TL at end of dam and pass café on RHS. Continue for descent.

18 Bear L downhill, following a narrow tarmac path by direction board showing yellow nature trail markers. Cross footbridge over river and TR. Continue to rejoin main road (B4393), where TR.

19 Continue on B4393, SP Llanfyllin.

20 Follow B4393 round sharp LH bend, steeply uphill, SP Llanfyllin.

21 TL at TJ, SP Llanfyllin. Continue past Globe garage on RHS. ***33.5km (21 miles)***

22 Immediately after garage, TL uphill into narrow lane – this is the start of another 5km (3 mile) climb, but it is not as severe as the first.

23 Reach top for long, fast descent. TAKE CARE! The road surface is poor in places, with substantial potholes which are often difficult to see in the shadow of the trees.

24 TR at TJ, no SP. ***42.5km (26.5 miles)***

25 TL at TJ onto A490, SP Llanfyllin. Continue into Llanfyllin.

26 TL opposite new style telephone box into Ffordd y Cain, no SP. This is start of the final long climb.

27 Keep R by red telephone box, SP

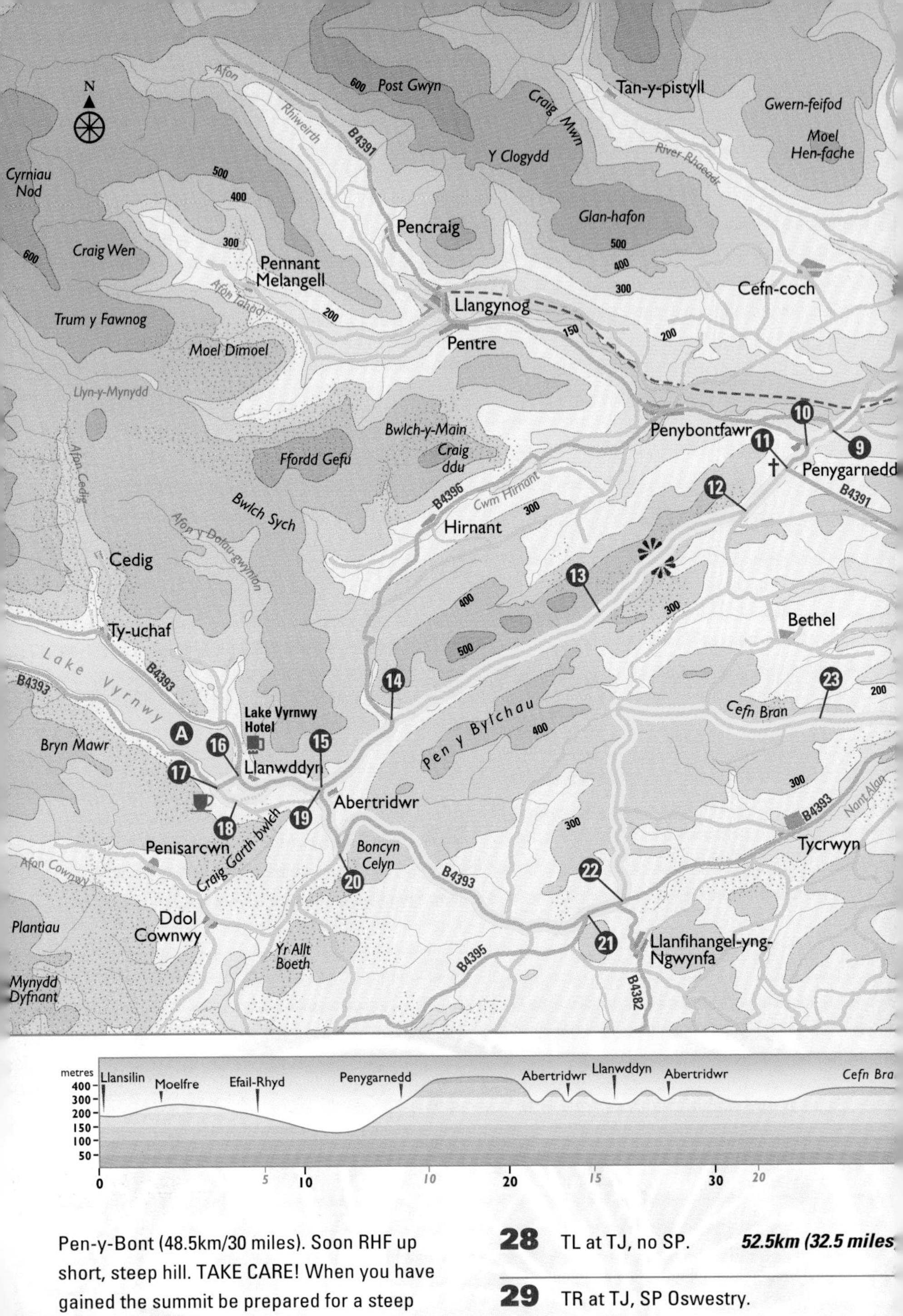

Pen-y-Bont (48.5km/30 miles). Soon RHF up short, steep hill. TAKE CARE! When you have gained the summit be prepared for a steep descent on a poor surface.

28 TL at TJ, no SP. ***52.5km (32.5 miles***

29 TR at TJ, SP Oswestry.

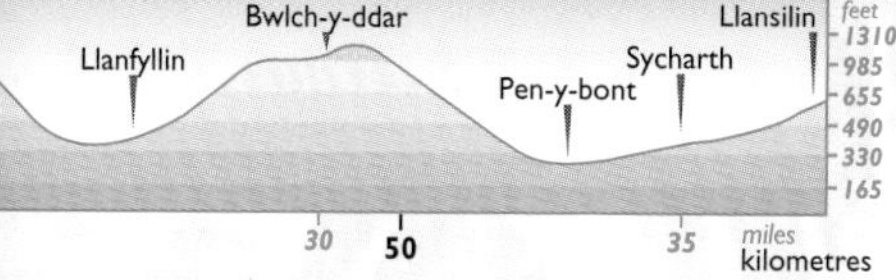

30 TL, SP Llansilin. Continue, following SP Llansilin.

31 TR up track, SP Footpath (57km/35.5 miles). To visit site of motte and bailey castle, park bike at black barn, go through gate and walk 100m to well preserved site.

Otherwise, continue SO.

32 TR at XR, SP Llansilin. Continue SO into Llansilin.

33 TR into car park to finish the ride.

59.5km (37 miles)

Route **17**

THE DENBIGH MOORS – LLANFAIR TALHAIARN AND PENTREFOELAS

Route information

Distance 61km (38 miles)

Grade Strenuous

Terrain A hilly route on tarmac. There are several climbs, one long and the others steep, but there are compensating long descents, particularly towards the end of the route. All the roads are normally quiet, even the A543 across the Denbigh Moors.

Time to allow 6–8 hours.

Getting there by car From the A55 at Abergele take the A548 south to Llanfair Talhaiarn, approximately 8km (5 miles) away. The car park is on the RHS, immediately after crossing the stone bridge in Llanfair Talhaiarn.

Getting there by train There is no practical rail access to this route.

This route closely follows the River Elwy and its tributaries, the Cledwyn and the Aled. Starting beside the River Elwy in Llanfair Talhaiarn, the route heads south west, following a narrow lane upstream through woodland for a short climb and a descent, crossing the River Cledwyn. The main route continues to climb to Gwytherin, with splendid views of Snowdonia. An alternative route is available here, following closer to the River Cledwyn along narrow and undulating lanes to Gwytherin over the same distance. From Gwytherin the route climbs up onto the Denbigh Moors (Hiraethog) to a height of 400m (1312.5 feet). On to Pentrefoelas, with the mountains of Snowdonia in view to the west. After a short spell on the A5 the route climbs back to the moors to Llyn Aled and the Aled Isaf Reservoir before a descent back to Llanfair Talhaiarn.

Places of interest along the route

A Llanfair Talhaiarn

A picturesque village on the banks of the River Elwy. The poet John Jones (1810–1869) is buried in the village.

B Gwytherin

In the hills of the Denbigh Moors. The churchyard contains a number of vertical stones several of which have Latin inscriptions and are believed to date from the 7th century. There are also some splendid and ancient yew trees.

C Rhaeadr y Bedd and the Aled Isaf Dam

Rhaeadr y Bedd was a popular destination for coach trips from the holiday resorts of north

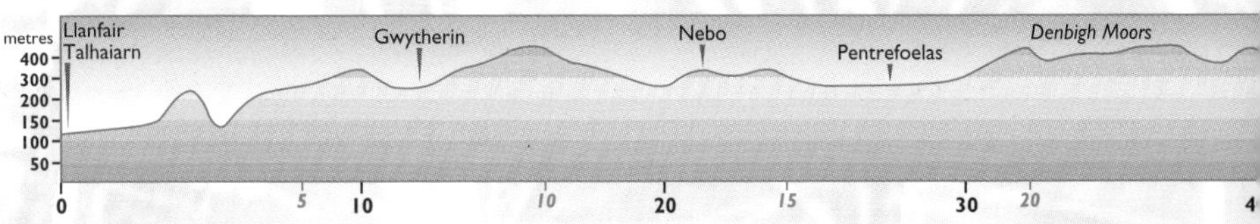

The mountains of Snowdonia

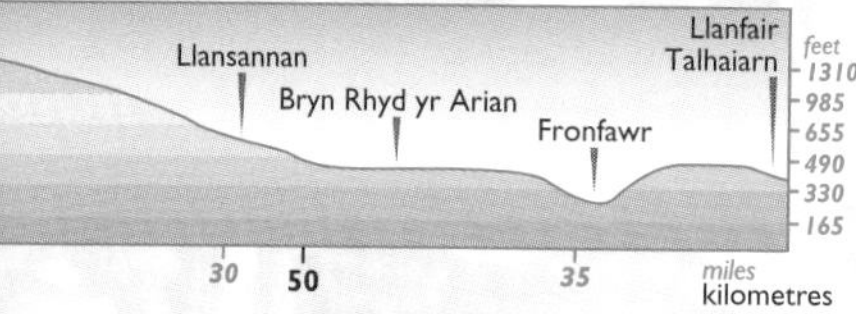

Wales before the Aled Isaf dam was built. The waterfall now only carries overflow water down from the reservoir into the Aled gorge after periods of heavy rain but it is still worth a visit.

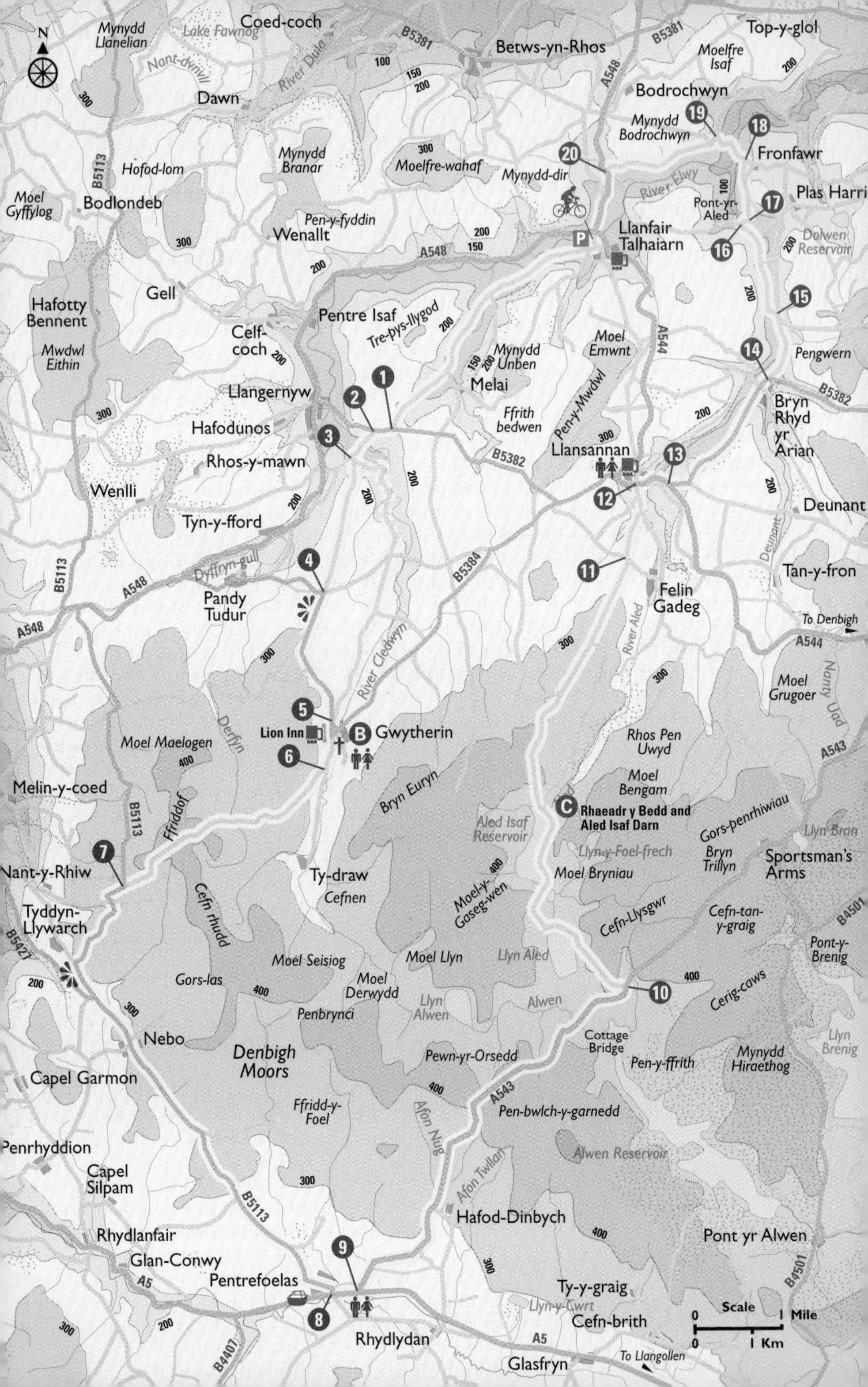

N
Mynydd Llanelian
Lake Fawnog
Coed-coch
B5381
Betws-yn-Rhos
B5381
Top-y-glol
Nant-dyvill
River Dulas
100
150
200
A548
Moelfre Isaf
200
300
Dawn
Bodrochwyn
Mynydd Bodrochwyn
19
18
Mynydd Branar
300
Moelfre-wahaf
Mynydd-dir
20
Fronfawr
B5113
Hofod-lom
River Elwy
100
Plas Harri
Moel Gyffylog
Bodlondeb
Pen-y-fyddin
Pont-yr-Aled
17
300
Wenallt
200
P
Llanfair Talhaiarn
Dolwen Reservoir
A548
150
16
200
200
Gell
Hafotty Bennent
Pentre Isaf
Tre-pys-llygod
200
200
15
Celf-coch
200
Moel Emwnt
A544
Mwdwl Eithin
Mynydd Unben
150
200
14
Pengwern
1
Melai
Pen-y-Mwdwl
B5382
Llangernyw
2
Bryn Rhyd yr Arian
Ffrith bedwen
200
300
Hafodunos
3
300
Llansannan
13
Rhos-y-mawn
B5382
200
200
200
12
200
Wenlli
Deunant
Tyn-y-fford
Deunant
4
B5384
11
Tan-y-fron
B5113
Dyffryn-gull
A548
Pandy Tudur
Felin Gadeg
River Aled
To Denbigh
A548
300
A544
300
300
River Cledwyn
Moel Grugoer
Nanty Uad
5
Lion Inn
B
Gwytherin
Derfyn
Moel Maelogen
Rhos Pen Uwyd
6
400
A543
Melin-y-coed
Moel Bengam
Bryn Euryn
Ffriddof
B5113
C
Rhaeadr y Bedd and Aled Isaf Darn
Aled Isaf Reservoir
Gors-penrhiwiau
Llyn Bran
7
Llyn-y-Foel-frech
Bryn Trillyn
Sportsman's Arms
Nant-y-Rhiw
Ty-draw
400
Moel Bryniau
Cefnen
Moel-y-Gaseg-wen
Tyddyn-Llywarch
Cefn rhudd
Cefn-Llysgwr
Cefn-tan-y-graig
B4501
B5427
Pont-y-Brenig
Moel Seisiog
Moel Llyn
Llyn Aled
200
400
Gors-las
400
Moel Derwydd
10
Cerig-caws
Llyn Alwen
Alwen
300
Penbrynci
Cottage Bridge
Llyn Brenig
Nebo
Denbigh Moors
Pewn-yr-Orsedd
Pen-y-ffrith
Mynydd Hiraethog
Capel Garmon
400
A543
Ffridd-y-Foel
Afon Nug
Pen-bwlch-y-garnedd
Penrhyddion
Alwen Reservoir
Capel Silpam
300
Afon Twllan
B5113
Hafod-Dinbych
Rhydlanfair
400
Pont yr Alwen
Glan-Conwy
9
300
B4501
A5
Pentrefoelas
Ty-y-graig
Llyn-y-Cwrt
8
Scale
0
1 Mile
300
200
Cefn-brith
Rhydlydan
A5
0
1 Km
B4407
To Llangollen
Glasfryn

Route description

Leave the car park in Llanfair Talhaiarn via the exit near the tennis courts and TR into a narrow lane to follow the river upstream.

1 TR at TJ onto B5382, SP Llangernyw, for steep descent. ***5.5km (3.5 miles)***

2 LHF, SP Gwytherin, and cross River Cledwyn.

3 For alternative route to Gwytherin, following close to River Cledwyn, TL after 100m, SP Pen Isaf. Continue along this narrow road, rejoining main route just before Gwytherin, continuing route at direction 5.

Otherwise, TL, SP Gwytherin, and continue steeply uphill.

4 SO at XR onto B5384, SP Gwytherin. ***9km (5.5 miles)***

5 SO through Gwytherin (Lion Inn on RHS, church on LHS).

6 TR steeply uphill, SP Pentrefoelas.

7 SO, SP Nebo/Pentrefoelas, and join B5113 (17.5km/11 miles). Continue along B5113 for approximately 10.5km (6.5 miles).

8 Arrive Pentrefoelas. TL onto A5, SP Llangollen. ***28km (17.5 miles)***

9 TL onto A543, SP Denbigh. Continue north on this road. Cross Cottage Bridge and continue for 1km (0.6 mile).

10 TL onto narrow lane, SP Llyn Aled (37km/23 miles). Continue, passing Aled Isaf Reservoir and Rhaeadr y Bedd.

11 TR after sharp LH bend (46.5km/29 miles), SP Llansannan, and descend steep hill into Llansanan.

12 TR at TJ onto A544, SP Dinbych (Denbigh).

13 TL at XR, SP Henllan B5382. Cross stone bridge and keep R through Bryn Rhydyr Arian.

14 LHF, SP Llannefydd.

15 TL at oblique XR (53km/33 miles), no SP. Continue steeply downhill to cross River Aled.

16 TR, no SP, and recross River Aled via Pont-yr-Aled stone bridge.

17 TL steeply uphill, no SP.

18 TL at TJ, SP Llanfair Talhaiarn, and cross River Elwy via bridge (Bont y Gwyddel).

19 TL at TJ, SP Llanfair Talhaiarn. ***57km (35.5 miles)***

20 TL at TJ, SP Llanfair Talhaiarn, and descend to return to car park and the end of the ride. ***61km (38 miles)***

Food and drink

Llanfair Talhaiarn and Llansannan have pubs providing food. There is also a post office and store in Pentrefoelas.

Lion Inn, Gwytherin

Offering drinks and meals (closed Mondays).

Route **18**

PWLLHELI AND THE LLEYN PENINSULA

Route information

Distance 62.5km (39 miles)

Grade Strenuous

Terrain Quiet and sometimes undulating roads for which low gears will be required.

Time to allow 4–8 hours.

Getting there by car Take the A499 from Caernarfon or the A497 from Portmadoc. There is car parking by the railway station.

Getting there by train Pwllheli is the western terminus of the Cambrian Coast line from Shrewsbury. Telephone (0345) 484950 for travel information.

This route is almost entirely on quiet country lanes, offering interesting views of Snowdonia, the Lleyn Peninsula and its coastline. From Pwllheli the route heads north west along the Saints Road. Turning south west, there is an optional visit to Porth Dinllaen on the northern coast of the Lleyn Peninsula, before the route heads back to the south coast and Porth Neigwl (also known as Hell's Mouth). From here more quiet country roads take you north east and back to Pwllheli.

Places of interest along the route

A Pwllheli

Popular with visitors, Pwllheli was a fishing town. Today the marina developed in the old harbour is a popular sailing centre. Market day is Wednesday. For further information contact the town's Tourist Information Centre on (01758) 613000.

B Porth Dinllaen

Situated on the north coast of the Lleyn Peninsula, Porth Dinllaen is a picturesque hamlet with a sandy bay and popular yacht anchorage.

C Plas Yn Rhiw, Rhiw

A small manor house restored by three sisters. The house is part medieval with Tudor and Georgian additions, and is surrounded by ornamental gardens. There are spectacular views across Cardigan Bay. National Trust property. Open March to October, Thursday–Monday 1200–1700; May to September also Wednesday 1200–1700. Charge. Telephone (01758) 780219.

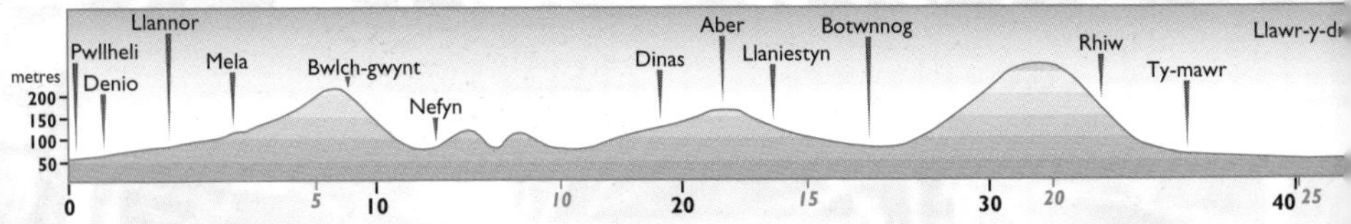

Food and drink

Plenty of choice in Pwllheli and there is a pub in Porth Dinllaen.

Bryn Cynan, near Nefyn
Bar meals available.

Tu Hwnt I'r Afon, Rhyd-y-clafdy
Offers bar meals.

Route description

TL out of Pwllheli station, into town centre and SO at mini roundabout. TR at second mini roundabout into Stryd Moch. Follow SP Coleg Meirion Dwyfor and climb steep hill to pass college. Continue to Llannor.

1 TR at TJ by church.

2 Take LHF. Then SO at next three small junctions to B4354.

3 Arrive B4354. SO WITH CARE at XR (6.5km/4 miles). Continue over Bwlch-gwynt (Windy Pass) and descend steeply to Pistyll.

4 TL at TJ onto B4417 (10km/6 miles). Continue to Nefyn.

5 SO at roundabout onto A497, SP Pwllheli.

6 To visit Porth Dinllaen, TR at roundabout and follow SP through Morfa Nefyn. After visit, retrace to roundabout and TR to rejoin route.

Otherwise, SO at roundabout, SP Dinas. SO at junction (16km/10 miles) and then SO at XR (Glan Rhyd), continuing towards Dinas.

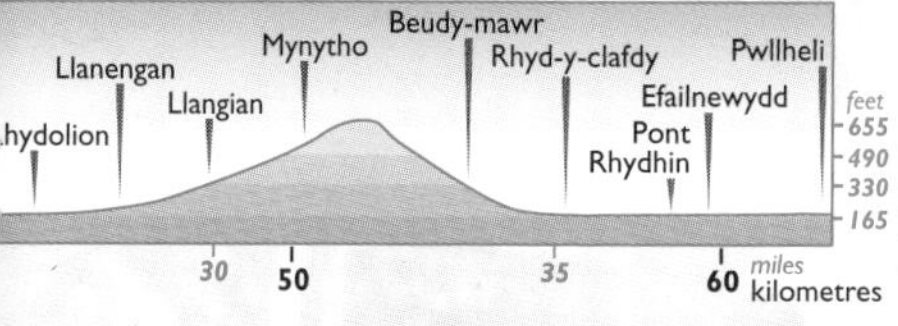

7 TL at junction (18.5km/11.5 miles). Continue into Dinas.

8 TR at TJ and continue to Llaniestyn.

9 SO up hill at junction (by village hall/church). ***21.5km (13.5 miles)***

10 TR at TJ, SP Botwnnog/Nanhoran.

11 Arrive Botwnnog. TL at TJ onto B4413, SP Llanbedrog/Pwllheli. ***25.5km (16 miles)***

12 TR at junction (by chapel), then SO uphill at junction. Continue SO at next three small junctions.

Plas Yn Rhiw

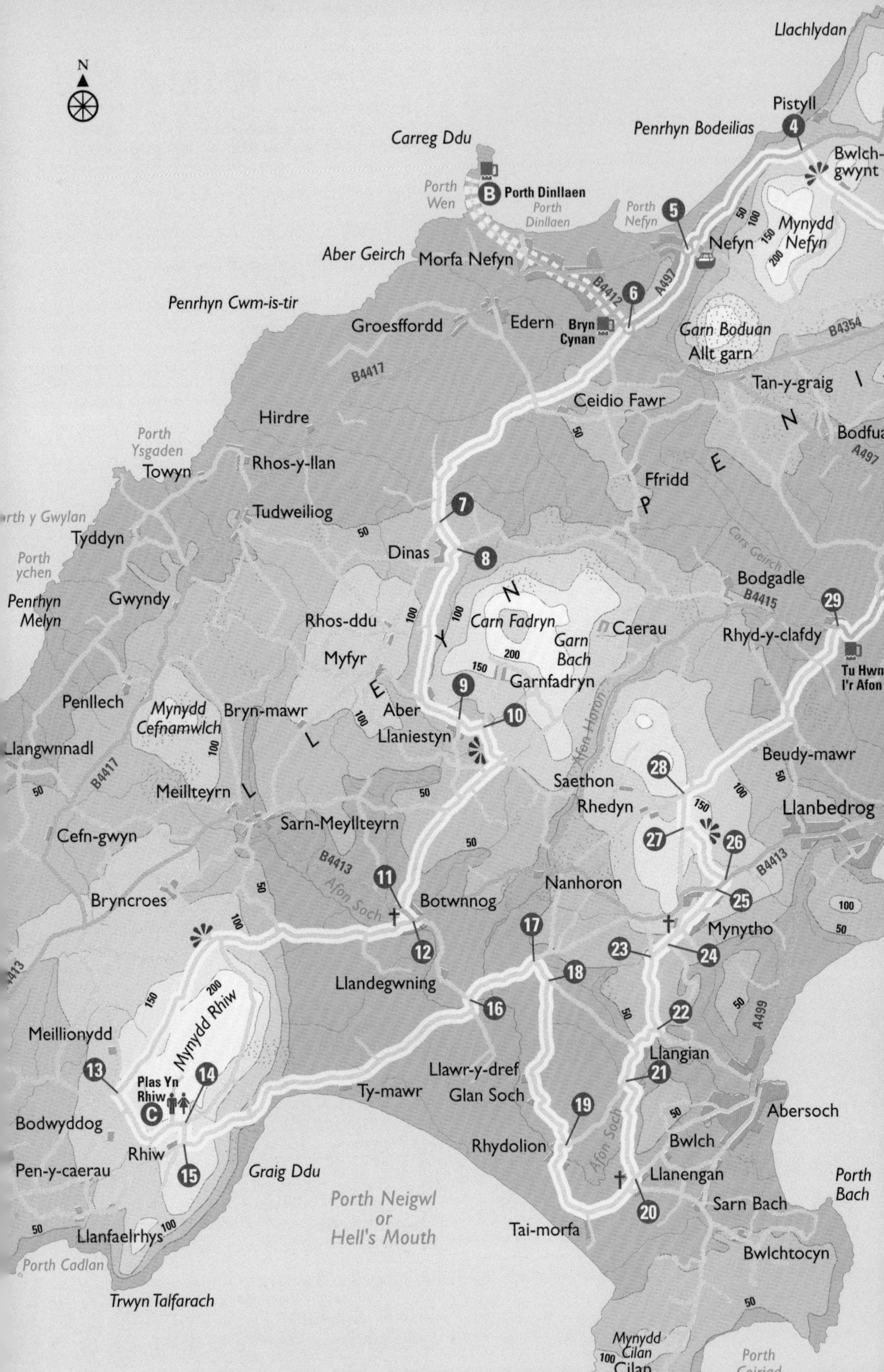
N
Llachlydan
Pistyll
Penrhyn Bodeilias
Bwlch-gwynt
Carreg Ddu
Porth Wen
Porth Dinllaen
Porth Dinllaen
Porth Nefyn
Nefyn
Mynydd Nefyn
Aber Geirch
Morfa Nefyn
Penrhyn Cwm-is-tir
Groesffordd
Edern
Bryn Cynan
Garn Boduan
Allt garn
B4412
A497
B4354
B4417
Tan-y-graig
Ceidio Fawr
Bodfuan
Hirdre
Porth Ysgaden
Towyn
Rhos-y-llan
Ffridd
Porth y Gwylan
Tudweiliog
Tyddyn
Porth ychen
Dinas
Cors Geirch
Bodgadle
B4415
Penrhyn Melyn
Gwyndy
Rhos-ddu
Carn Fadryn
Caerau
Rhyd-y-clafdy
Garn Bach
Myfyr
Garnfadryn
Tu Hwnt I'r Afon
Penllech
Mynydd Cefnamwlch
Bryn-mawr
Aber
Llaniestyn
Afon Horon
Llangwnnadl
Beudy-mawr
Saethon
Meillteyrn
Rhedyn
Llanbedrog
Sarn-Meyllteyrn
Cefn-gwyn
B4413
Afon Soch
Nanhoron
Bryncroes
Botwnnog
Mynytho
Llandegwning
A499
Mynydd Rhiw
Meillionydd
Llangian
Plas Yn Rhiw
Llawr-y-dref
Ty-mawr
Glan Soch
Abersoch
Bodwyddog
Rhydolion
Bwlch
Rhiw
Pen-y-caerau
Graig Ddu
Llanengan
Porth Bach
Porth Neigwl or Hell's Mouth
Sarn Bach
Llanfaelrhys
Tai-morfa
Bwlchtocyn
Porth Cadlan
Trwyn Talfarach
Mynydd Cilan
Cilan Uchaf
Porth Ceiriad
Trwyn-y-Fulfran
L L E Y N P E N I

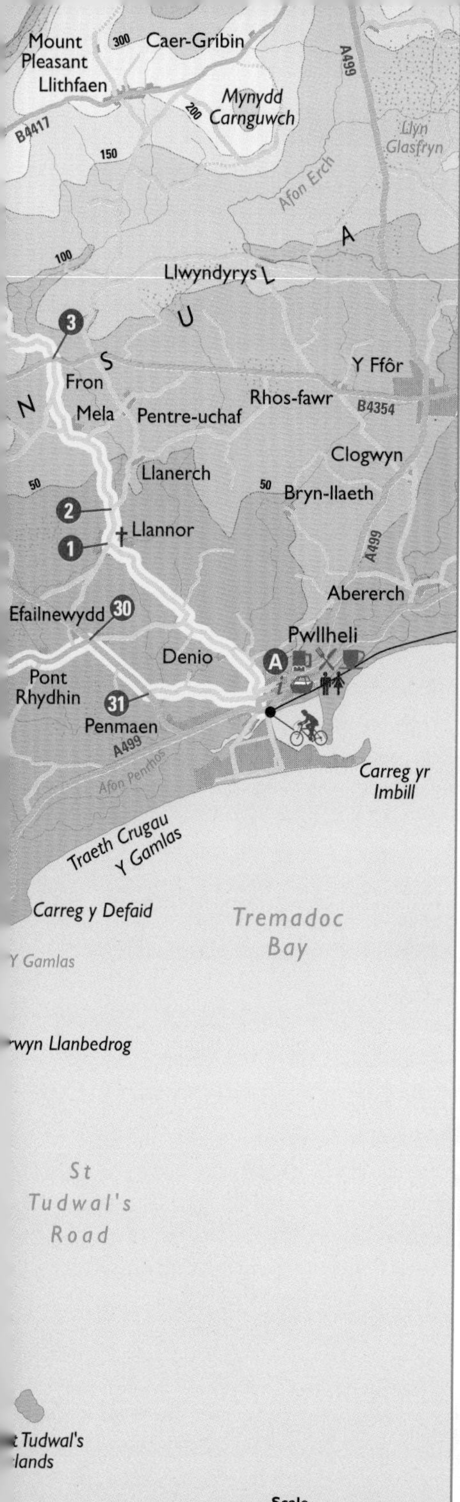

13 TL at TJ and continue up hill (32km/ 20 miles). SO at next junction.

14 To visit Plas Yn Rhiw, TL at TJ.

Otherwise, TR at TJ, SP Aberdaron.

15 TL at TJ, SP Abersoch/Pwllheli, for steep descent. Continue along this road.

16 RHF, SP Mynytho/Abersoch.

17 TR at TJ, SP Llangian/Llanengan/Hell's Mouth. ***40km (25 miles)***

18 TR at TJ, no SP.

19 TR at TJ, cross bridge and follow road to Llanengan.

20 TL at TJ (by church) in Llanengan , SP Llangian/Aberdaron (45.5km/28.5 miles). Continue into Llangian.

21 SO at junction by church hall and climb.

22 TL at TJ, SP Mynytho.

23 TR at junction, SP Mynytho/Pwllheli.

24 Pass chapel (50km/31 miles) and take RHF through Mynytho.

25 TR at TJ onto B4413, SP Pwllheli.

26 TL at junction. (After 100m, between house and bungalow, pass ruined windmill. Walk to windmill for good views.)

27 TR at TJ, no SP. ***52km (32.5 miles)***

28 TR at TJ, SP Rhydyclafty, for long descent into Rhydyclafty.

29 TR at TJ onto B4415, SP Pwllheli (56km/35 miles). Continue into Efailnewydd.

30 TR at TJ onto A497.

31 TL at junction (before arrows for bend). Follow road into Pwllheli where TR at XR into Stryd Moch. TL at mini roundabout and return to station to complete the ride.

62.5km (39 miles)

Route **19**

LLANUWCHLLYN AND DOLGELLAU

Route information

Distance 62.5km (39 miles)

Grade Strenuous

Terrain Mostly single tracked roads, often hilly, twisty and unfenced. The surfaces are generally good but may have a covering of stones and mud after wet weather. There are many gates and cattle grids on the route but it is virtually traffic free away from the A roads. This is compensated for by the large number of sheep that inhabit the area – watch out for them.

Time to allow 6–7 hours.

Getting there by car Llanuwchllyn is at the south end of Bala Lake, off the A494. From Bala turn left off the A494 onto the B4403, SP Llangower and continue through Llanuwchllyn, pass turning for narrow gauge railway on LHS and after 200m arrive at a car park, the start of the ride.

Getting there by train There is no practical rail access to this route.

From Llanuwchllyn the route heads west across Snowdonia, and then south to Dolgellau, with an optional visit to the Mawddach Estuary. The route then heads north east back through Snowdonia National Park to Llanuwchllyn. The route takes in a wide range of scenery, from pastoral scenes and open moors among the mountains to forest roads and the Mawddach Estuary. It is beautiful and the views from the tops of the hills are quite outstanding and make all the effort worthwhile. Remember to look back as you stop to catch your breath, or you will miss the scenery behind you. As in most mountainous areas, the weather can be fickle, changing rapidly several times a day. It is essential, therefore, that waterproofs are carried no matter how settled the weather looks when you start out. You should also carry food and drink to sustain you during the ride.

Places of interest along the route

A Llanuwchllyn

A small village at the southern end of Bala Lake. The Bala Lake Railway runs between Llanuwchllyn and Bala. For further details see route 3.

B Mawddach Estuary

There is a RSPB nature reserve on the edge of the Mawddach Estuary, together with a flat cycle/pedestrian track on the bed of the defunct Barmouth to Ruabon railway, now part

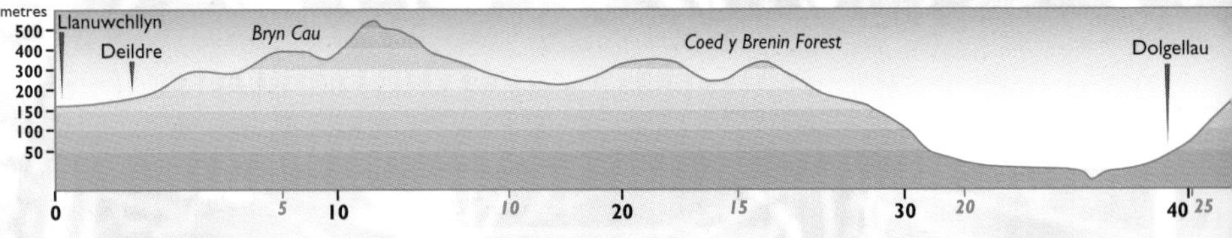

Bala Lake

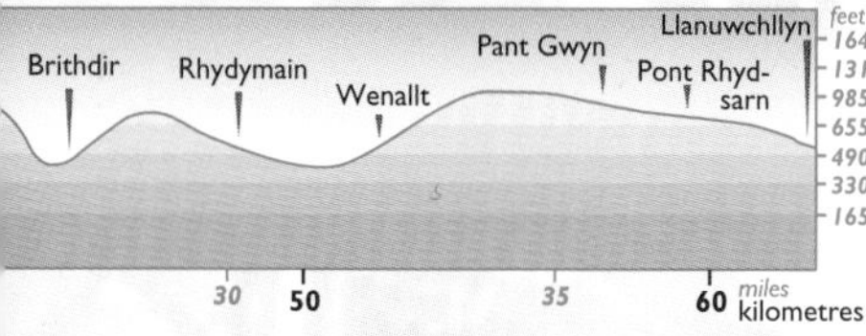

of the National Cycle Route. The signal box at the reserve's car park is used as an observatory for bird watching. The trail is 14km (8.5 miles) long and is worth exploring if you have the time and the energy to ride all or part of it.

N
A4212
Trawsfynydd
Prysor
Moel Llyfnant
Moel
Foel Boeth
Moel-Oernant
Bryn Cau
Llyn Gelligain
Moel Ddu
Moel y Feidiog
Afon
A470
Bronaber
Afon Gain
Mynydd Bach
Nant Hir
Mynydd Bryn-llech
Pont-y-Grible
Nant-y-Groerm
Afon Bryn-llin-fa
Cerig Chwibanog
Craig-y-Pen-maen
Afon Cwmhesgen
Llyn Crych-y-waen
Cerig yr Iwrch
Afon Crawew
Afon Eden
Afon Mawddach
Rhobell y Big
Moel Gron
Dduallt
Afon Dyfrd
Craig Aberserw
Coed y Brenin Forest
Moel Hafod Owen
Afon Ceit
Carreg Lusog
Cefndeuddwr
Rhobell Fawr
Afon Camlan
Craig-y-Benglog
Foel Du
Ganllwyd
Cerniau
Afon Wen
Moel Cors-y-garnedd
Afon Melau
Craig Cau
Wenallt
Garn
Llanfachreth
Nannau-is afon
Nannau-uwch-afon
Afon Las or Afon Babi
Cwm Gwnm
Rhydymain
Llyn Cynwch
Nannau
Afon Celyn
Bont Newydd
Llanelltyd
A496
A494
Mawddach Estuary
B4416
Toll
Brithdir
Bwlch-y-Figyn
A493
enmaenpool
Afon Wnion
A470
Dolgellau
Camlan
Cross Foxes Inn
Craig-y-Bwlch
Gilfachwydd
Llyn Gwernan
River Aran
A487
Afon Ceri

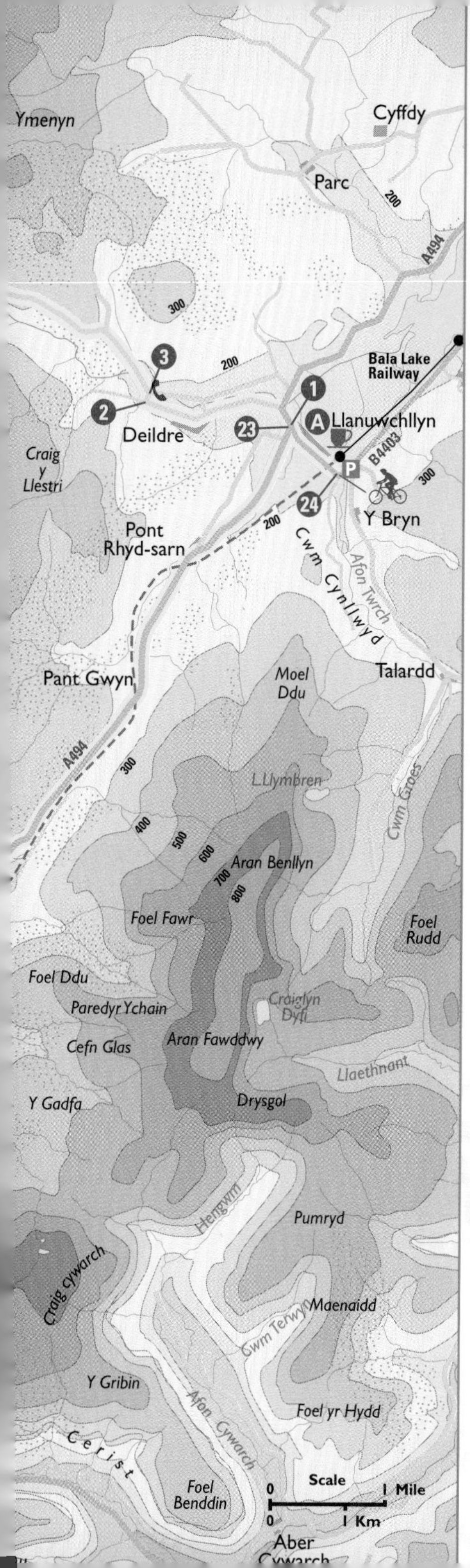

Free access at all reasonable times. Telephone the Snowdonia National Park Visitor Centre (see below) for more information.

C Dolgellau

A market town and administrative centre, Dolgellau means 'meadow of the hazels' and a Welsh parliament was held here in 1404 by Owain Glyndwr. The River Aran divides the town, which is linked by a 17th-century arched bridge. The Snowdonia National Park Visitor Centre, telephone (01341) 422888, is situated here and houses an exhibition on the surrounding area.

Route description

TR out of Llanuwchllyn car park and continue SO through village.

1 TR at TJ with A494, SP Bala. Then TL immediately before bridge, no SP.

2 TR opposite SP No Through Road. Continue and cross bridge.

3 TL (after crossing bridge, by telephone box), SP Trawsfynydd (3.5km/2 miles). Continue to cross cattle grid from where there is a series of five gates, some or all of which are likely to be shut. These are followed by two more cattle grids. TAKE CARE if the cloud is down on the road as some of the gates are part way down descents and will not be easy to see. Continue on this road for approximately 12km (7.5 miles) and cross bridge.

4 TL (after crossing bridge), SP Trawsfynydd. ***16km (10 miles)***

5 TL at TJ, SP Abergeirw/Dolgellau/Llanfachfreth.

6 Cross bridge over Afon Gain, then another cattle grid.

7 SO, SP Abergeirw/Dolgellau (19.5km/12 miles). Continue to cross four more cattle grids – the fourth is followed by an acute RH bend after a blind down hill approach so TAKE CARE!

8 TR at Y junction, SP Dolgellau.

24km (15 miles)

9 Cross bridge (by telephone box), SP Llanfachfreth/Dolgellau.

10 TR (sharply) at XR, SP Ty'n-y-groes (31.5km/19.5 miles), for steep descent.

11 TL at foot of hill (picnic site on LHS), SP Llanelltyd – this is a good place to stop for a meal break. Continue downhill through the lovely valley of the River Mawddach.

12 TR at TJ, no SP. ***35.5km (22 miles)***

13 TL at TJ onto A470 – you can now expect heavy traffic.

14 To visit Mawddach Estuary/Nature Reserve, TR onto A493, SP Tywyn, and continue to estuary. After visit, retrace route to A470 and TR to continue the route.

Otherwise, continue SO.

15 Take LHF, SP Dolgellau.

16 TR, SP Town Centre. Then take LHF (RHF SP No Entry) and TL into Arran Road.

17 TR uphill into Fron Serth (39.5km/24.5 miles). This is a long (2.5km/1.5 miles) and severe climb which you can avoid by going SO to junction with A470 where TR and rejoin the route at direction 19 to TL onto B4416, SP Brithdir. You will have a less severe climb but there may be heavy traffic.

18 TL (by new style telephone box), no SP.

19 TL onto A470, no SP, for 150m. Then TR onto B4416, SP Brithdir.

20 Arrive LH blind bend. TR (effectively SO) WITH CARE by telephone box, no SP.

45km (28 miles)

21 Pass telegraph pole with street light mounted on it (a rare sight around here) and immediately TR uphill, no SP, for another series of gates and cattle grids. (This turn occurs on a RH bend as the road is descending quickly – it is easy to miss the turn unless you are alert. If you do miss it, you will arrive at the A494 earlier than planned, in which case TR and pick up the route further along).

22 TR onto A494 (52km/32.5 miles), no SP, and continue on A494.

23 TR onto B4403, SP Llangower.

24 TL into car park to finish the ride.

62.5km (39 miles)

Food and drink

There is nowhere along the route for refreshment until you reach Dolgellau (cafés, tearooms and hotels) so you should carry food and drink with you. The same lack of refreshment facilities applies to the return trip, but the terrain is much kinder. All the same it is advisable to fill your water bottle in Dolgellau, especially in hot weather. There is a café at Llanuwchllyn station (open when trains are running, closes at 1700) and there are several cafés and hotels in Bala.

Route **20**

FLINTSHIRE – MOLD AND THE HALKYNS

Route information

Distance 62km (38.5 miles)

Grade Strenuous

Terrain With little flat riding, this route could be a serious challenge to the unfit cyclist. Low gears will help substantially. All the lanes used are quiet, even on summer Bank Holidays.

Time to allow 6–12 hours.

Getting there by car Mold is easily reached from the A55 and the A49. There is a large pay and display car park behind Somerfield supermarket, just south west of the traffic lights at XR on the High Street.

Getting there by train The nearest railway station is at Penyfford. Telephone (0345) 484950 for travel information. The round trip to Mold and back to the station is 4km (2.5 miles). To reach the start of the route, TR sharply out of station onto A5114 and pass under railway bridge. TR between telephone box and white cottage. TR at TJ, cross disused railway railway bridge. TL at TJ onto A5118 (no SP) and continue into Llong. TL in Llong (opposite stonemason). Cross bridge. TR then immediately TL over staggered XR, SP Ruthin. SO at roundabout, SP Mold/B54444. Then SO at traffic lights leading to High Street and start route at direction 1.

From Mold the route dips in and out of the deep valley of the Rivers Alyn and Wheeler, heading north to the Halkyns. These hills, scarred by centuries of mining, are seldom visited but offer a lofty view north over the Wirral and south to the Clwydian Hills. The roads in the Halkyns are exposed and windy, so wrap up warm in winter. Loose sheep on the moors can be more of a hazard than cars! The route then heads south east and returns to Mold downhill on quiet lanes. Note that some signposts are bilingual and often show the Welsh first. However, many of the rural junctions have no priority road markings or signposts; where there are signs, they often face the wrong direction. Trust the map and directions first, then fall back on the signposts.

Route description

Take car park exit that runs past toilets, TR at TJ (opposite Indian Restaurant), SP Queensferry A541, for 200m then TL at traffic lights into High Street.

1 Continue along High Street and SO at traffic lights. LHF by chapel/war memorial (Pwll Glas), SP Gwernaffield. TL at TJ (effectively SO) along Gwernaffield Road. Take RHF at top of bank SP 7T Restriction/Llyn-y-pandy/Rhydymwyn.

2 Ignoring lanes on LHS, descend to works where TL. Follow lane, passing between gateposts, alongside River Alyn.

6km (3.5 miles)

3 TR sharply by entrance to Coed Du Nursing Home. Continue for 200m past farm buildings.

Gwaenysgor
Meliden
Llanasa
Glan-yr-afon
Mostyn Quay
Red Lion
Mostyn
Gop Hill
Axton
Trelogan
Trelawnyd
Marian
Berthengam
Graig Fawr
Glan-y-don
Dyserth
Maen Achwyfan
Whitford (Chwitffford)
Downrig
Pwllhalog
Llyn Helyg
Mertyn
Greenfield (Maes-Glas)
Rock Inn
Carmel
Holway
Cwm
Bryn Glas
Lloc
Gorsedd
The Friary
Pantasaph
Holywell (Treffynnon)
Smithy Arms
Pen-y-cefn
Rhuallt
Brynford
Holywell Common
Babell
Glan Clwyd
Tremeirchion
Caerwys
Brynbella
Llannerch
Graig
Maes-mynan
Fox Inn
Afon-wen
Lixwm
Crown Inn
Rhes-y-cae
Walwen
Afonwen Craft & Antique Centre
Ddol
Ysceifiog
Vale of Clwyd
River Clwyd
River Wheeler
Pistyll
Bodfari
Geinas
Nannerch
Waen Aberwheeler
Colomendy
Hendre
Pentre-mawr
Denbigh (Dinbych)
Llangwyfan
Waen
Brookhouse
Rhiwbebyll
Cilcain
Pentre'r-felin
Llandyrnog
Ffordd-las
Ysradisat
Pentre
Hen-efail
Llanrhaeadr
Llangynhafal
Ffrith Mountain
Scale
Mile
Km
Llanwog
Hendrerwydd
Pentre Llanrhaeadr
Llanynys
Gellifor
A547
A548
A5151
A5026
A55
B5429
B5122
B5121
A541
A525
A543
Mold
Lixwm
Ysceifiog
Ddol
Afon-wen
Maes-mynan
Rhuallt
Dyserth
Llanasa
metres

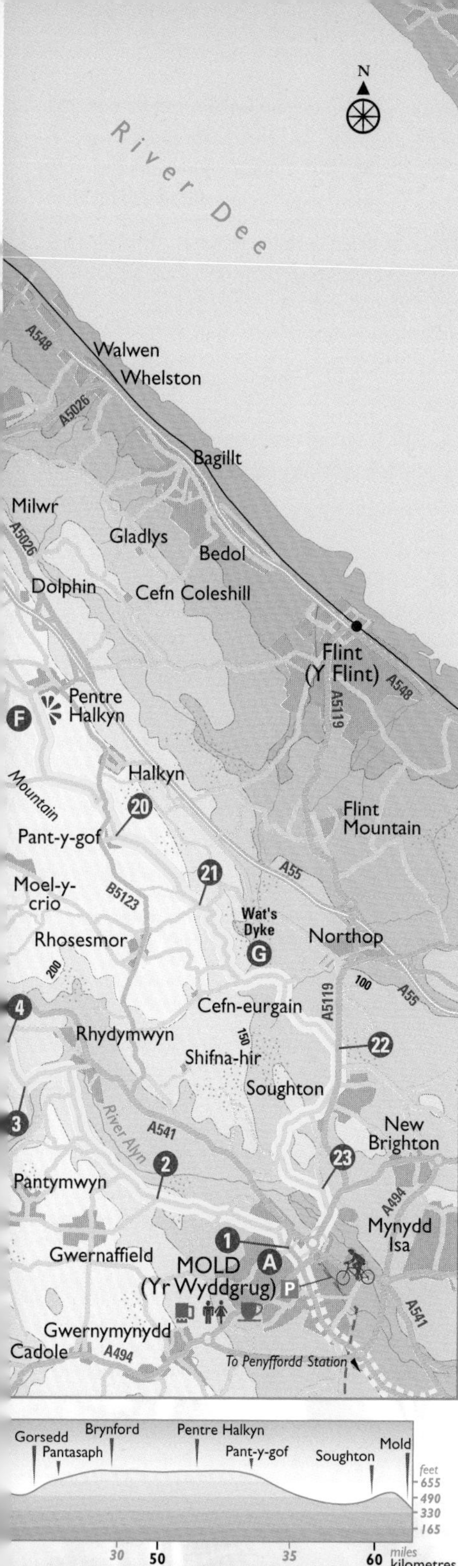

4 TL for climb, SP 3T Restriction. Ignore tracks on both sides. On descent, TR by post box and continue downhill. TR at staggered XR, no SP (but Moel Famau is visible, half-left with a pimple-like shelter on summit).

5 TR at TJ.

6 Arrive XR with busy A541. SO WITH CARE, SP Rhes-y-cae. Continue for 300m and TL under power lines, SP Unsuitable for HGVS (10km/ 6 miles). Continue to TJ, ignoring lane on LHS and tracks to L and R.

7 TL at TJ along Fford y Graig, SP Lixwm. TR at XR into Lixwm (13.5km/8.5 miles). Pass Crown Inn and:

8 TL into Fford Gledlon. TL at TJ and pass between church and chapel in Ysceifiog village. Pass Fox Inn on RHS. Keep SO, SP Afonwen (Restricted). Descend steeply on slippery, gravely lane. TL sharply at bottom of very steep section – do not cross bridge by stone mill building. TR at TJ onto A541 and pass Afonwen Craft and Antique Centre on LHS (18km/ 11 miles). Continue along A541 for 1km (0.6 mile), passing an exceptionally handsome horse trough on LHS by junction with Caerwys Road.

9 TR just before entrance to Maes Mynan Hall. TL by quarry gates, no SP, and climb steeply. Occasional glimpses can be had over hedgerows towards Vale of Clwyd.

21.5km (13.5 miles)

10 SO at XR and head under power lines. TL at TJ and almost immediately TR (before losing much height), SP pointing in wrong direction so ignore!

11 TR at TJ under power lines (Offa's Dyke meets road on LHS). TL at XR, no SP (but yellow grit bin). Descend quickly, ignoring turning on RHS, and SO into No Through Road. You will need to brake hard at bollards at foot of hill. Cross A55 via footbridge and go down zig zagged path. Remount for final dip. TL at TJ to arrive in Rhuallt. ***26km (16 miles)***

12 TR at XR by Smithy Arms. Follow road uphill (views of castles at Denbigh, Bodelwyddan and Rhuddlan and tower at Henllan Church; you can see the coast line from Prestatyn, Rhyl, Abergele and Colwyn Bay to the Orme on a fine day). Ignore lanes to L and R, pass Pentre Cwm manor house and continue into Dyserth for 400m beyond SP 30MPH. ***30km (18.5 miles)***

13 RHF (after phone box on LHS). Continue through back streets of Dyserth. SO at XR (Pandy Lane) and take RHF across disused railway (now a cycleway/footpath). TL at TJ then almost immediately TR at TJ (32km/20 miles). Entrance to Graig Fawr is almost directly in front of you as you make this turn – the highest part of the hill (and the best views along coast) is reached on foot via stile from car park drive.

14 Follow lane as it climbs away from Graig Fawr. SO at XR, SP Llanasa, and continue into Llanasa. TR by Red Lion pub, SP Trelogan, for steady climb. SO at XR, SP Whitford (views across Dee Estuary to Wirral peninsula and Hilbre Island). ***38km (23.5 miles)***

15 TL at TJ, SP Mostyn. Maen Achwyfan Cross is in field on RHS, access via kissing gate.

16 Continue along this road to bear R around field containing cross (ignoring two TL). Then TL, SP Holywell/Caerwys. TL at roundabout, SP Holywell A5026. Continue into Lloc. ***42km (26 miles)***

17 SO at XR by Rock Inn, along one way street. TL at TJ for short climb into Gorsedd. On descent, TR at XR by church, SP Friary.

18 TL into Monastery Road, SP Friary. Pass friary on LHS, derelict nunnery on RHS. Continue as road bridges A55 and crosses golf course. ***46km (28.5 miles)***

19 TR at XR, SP Lixwm (47.5km/29.5 miles). TL at TJ (Fford Groes), SP Rhes-y-cae. Continue through open cast areas (view on LHS over Deeside and New Dee Bridge). Take RHS on descent, SP Windmill. TL at TJ (masts directly ahead on hill). Take RHF (by SP 7T Access). TR at TJ and take LHF opposite Blue Bell Inn. ***52.5km (32.5 miles)***

20 TL at TJ, passing stagnant pool on RHS. Enjoy descent, ignoring tracks and lanes on both sides. Next turn is easy to miss – on a particularly fast downhill section TR sharply by house, SP 3T Limit. ***53.5km (33 miles)***

21 TL at unmarked TJ and continue descent. Take LHF (with priority), still descending. A short section of Wat's Dyke is visible to the discerning eye. Then take RHF (pond below to left). ***55.5km (34.5 miles)***

22 TR at TJ onto A5119, no SP. TR at Cross Keys XR in Sychdyn (Soughton), for fast downhill and TL, no SP. ***59.5km (37 miles)***

23 TR at TJ by Civic Centre, then TR at TJ, SP Mold A5119. SO at roundabout (actually third exit including supermarket entrance) along King Street, SP Town Centre. TL at traffic lights into High Street. To return to car park, TR at XR (traffic lights) then TL into car park to complete the route. ***62km (38.5 miles)***

To return to Penyffordd station, SO XR (traffic lights) along Wrexham Street. SO at roundabout, SP Wrexham B5444. SO at staggered XR, no SP, and continue into Llong. TR at TJ in Llong. TR at staggered XR (by SP Golf Course). Take LHF by fourth bridge and TL at TJ (by telephone box). Continue under railway bridge and TL sharply to reach the station.

Places of interest along the route

Ⓐ Mold

The county town of Flintshire and birthplace of Daniel Owen, the Welsh Dickens. The town library has an exhibition on his life. The 15th-century St Mary's Church contains interesting stained glass and the remains of a Norman motte and bailey can be see at Bailey Hill. To the north west of Mold is the River Alyn, a tributary of the Dee. The section followed on the route often dries up in the summer as it enters sink holes further upstream. Contact Mold Tourist Information Centre for further information on (01352) 759331.

B Afonwen Craft and Antique Centre, Afonwen

A diverse collection of local arts and crafts with a café housed in an old flax mill. Open all year, Tuesday–Sunday and Bank Holiday Mondays 0930–1730. Admission free. Telephone (01352) 720965.

C Dyserth and Graig Fawr

Dyserth has a pretty waterfall best seen from below. Nominal charge. Graig Fawr is a Site of Special Scientific Interest owned by the National Trust and its limestone soils support rare plants and butterflies. There are commanding views over the coastal plain and the Vale of Clwyd. Free access (on foot only) at all reasonable times. Telephone Prestatyn Tourist Information Centre for further information on (01745) 889092.

D Maen Achwyfan, near Whitford

At least 1000 years old, this ancient cross was probably a boundary marker. It is carved in a Viking style. Free access at all reasonable times.

E The Friary, Pantasaph

A working friary and derelict nunnery (across the road) attracting many pilgrims to its shrines. You may be lucky and get a cup of tea and a cold snack in the tearoom, although opening hours are sporadic. Telephone Prestatyn Tourist Information Centre for more information.

F The Halkyns

A little travelled range of hills, scarred by lead and limestone workings. There are miles of tunnels underground, and even an old railway. Much of the land is unenclosed and there are numerous capped mining shafts visible on the surface. Superb views sweep as far away as Blackpool Tower over the Wirral peninsula and Liverpool, and south to the Clwydian Hills and the Berwyns beyond. It can get cold and windy up here.

G Wat's Dyke

The more easterly of the two defensive banks and the shorter at 61.5km (38 miles) long, said to have been built in antiquity to separate England from Wales. It can be seen best from this location, as a raised field margin topped with mature trees. The other bank, Offa's Dyke, is much more pronounced on the ground and has lent its name to a long distance footpath.

Food and drink

Mold is well served by pubs and cafés, although most places close on Sundays. When there is no other choice, try Binelli's on King Street. Dyserth offers a selection of spit and sawdust pubs, a convenience store and fish and chip shop. There is a café at Afonwen Craft and Antiques Centre. There are also a few village stores en route but they rarely seem to be open – take pot luck here!

Fox Inn, Ysceifiog

Open all day, every day for morning coffee, food and drink.

Smithy Arms, Rhuallt

On Offa's Dyke path and used to supplying drinks, snacks and meals to outdoor types.

Red Lion, Llanasa

Offers food and drink every day, although it can get busy on Sundays.

Rock Inn, Lloc

Excellent pub serving real ales and value for money bar meals (food available 1200–1400 and 1800–2100).

Route 21

CONWY AND BETWS-Y-COED

Route information

Distance 74km (46 miles)

Grade Strenuous

Terrain Many short, steep ascents and descents and three long, hard hills, well worth the effort for the incomparable views.

Time to allow 6–8 hours.

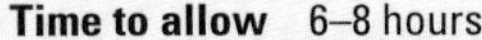

Getting there by car Conwy is easily reached from the A55. The Castle, which visibly dominates the town, has a mini roundabout adjacent to it – from here take the B5106, SP Trefriw. Go through old town wall, with castle on LHS, then under rail bridge and follow road to right, past Billington's Garage, for 200m. There is a pay and display car park on RHS.

Getting there by train Conwy station is not easy to use – just one rail company stops at the station, and then only by request. Telephone (0345) 484950 for travel information. If you alight at Conwy Station, TL out of station into one way system. Go through town wall and immediately TR into Town Ditch Road, re-enter town through wall, continue SO to mini roundabout by castle and proceed as above. You may want to use Llandudno station, approximately 1km (0.6 mile) from the start of the route, in which case TL out of station (by Kwik Save store) for 400m and SO at roundabout. Continue over causeway and bridge towards castle and continue from mini roundabout as above.

This is the most strenuous route in this guide. From Conwy the route heads south to cross the A5 and climbs sharply over a hill dividing the Rivers Conwy and Machno for a steep descent into Betwys. The return route follows the valley floor for a short way before heading west into the hills and back to Conwy. Much of the route uses two waymarked cycleways, but some of the signs may be missing or obscured by foliage so follow the route description carefully.

Places of interest along the route

A Conwy

A picturesque walled town on the banks of the River Conwy. **Conwy Castle** was built high above the Conwy estuary by Edward I between 1283 and 1289. There are magnificent views from the battlements. Cadw (Welsh Historic Monuments) site. Open daily, April to mid-May and October 0930–1700; mid-May to September 0930–1800; November to March, Monday–Saturday only 0930–1600. Charge. Telephone (01492) 592358. Although known principally for the magnificent castle, there are many other places of interest in and around the town, including Plas Mawr, Aberconwy House, Thomas Telford's suspension bridge, a butterfly park, aquatic centre, rare breeds farm and teapot museum. Contact the Tourist Information Centre for further information on (01492) 592248.

B Penmachno Woollen Mill, near Betws-y-coed

Visitors can learn about the weaving process and see Penmachno rugs being manufactured.

Café. Open all year, daily 1000–1730. Admission free. Telephone (01690) 710545.

C Ty Mawr

This was the birthplace of Bishop William Morgan, who first translated the entire Bible into Welsh. National Trust property with limited opening times. Telephone (01690) 760213 for details.

D Betwys-y-coed

A small town at the confluence of the Rivers Llugwy and Conwy. There are craft and outdoor equipment shops and many eateries. The **Motor Museum**, created from a private collection, houses over 30 motor vehicles and motoring memorabilia. Open Easter to October, daily 1000–1800. Charge. Telephone (01690) 710760. The **Conwy Valley Railway Museum** is located in the old goods yard. The museum contains signalling, train layouts and working models and offers rides on a miniature steam railway. Café. Open Easter to October, daily 1015–1700; November to Easter, weekends 1015–1600.

E Trefriw Woollen Mills, Trefriw

The mills are powered by electricity generated by their own water powered turbines and the turbines are open to visitors. Also demonstrations of hand spinning and a weaver's garden. Open Easter to October, Monday–Friday 0930–1730 (winter 1700); Saturday 1000–1700. Telephone (01492) 640462.

F Dolgarrog Memorial

Stop by the roadside to see the memorial, fixed to boulders carried down by the flood, to those killed when a dam in the hills above Dolgarrog collapsed.

Betws-y-coed

N
Penmaen-bach Point
Conwy Marsh
Esgyryn
Colwyn Bay
A55
Mochdre
Old Colwyn
Llanddulas
Conwy Mountain A547
Conwy
Conwy Castle
River Conwy
Llandudno Junction
Mynydd
Glyn
Llysfaen
Dwygyfylchi
Capelulo
Crows Nest
Gyffin
Hendre
Dolywd
Pantygloch
Meifod
Llanelian-yn-Rhôs
Genfrom
Bryn-y-maen
Ty-newydd
Foel Lus
Penmaenmawr
Tyn-y-ffridd
Llechwedd
Llansanffraid Glan Conwy
Ffriddy Mynydd
Plas-uchaf
B5381
B5113
B5383
A547
A470
B5106
B5279
Baclaw
Henryd
Pentrefelin
Dolwen
Coed-coch
Glan-yr-afon
Bryn Denwydd
Moelfre
Nant y Pandy
Mynydd Llanelian
Lake Fawnog
Betws-yn-Rhos
Nant-dywll
River Dulas
Afon Maes-y-bryn
Afon Ddu
Tal-y-fan
Hen-efoil
Ty'n Twll
Dawn
Rowen
Ty'n-y-groes
Graig
Hofod-lom
Mynydd Branar
Moelfre-wahaf
Bwlch-y-Ddeufaen
Brymbo
Moel Gyffylog
Bodlondeb
Tal-y-cafn
Drosgl
Hafitty-gwyn
Afon Roe
Pontwgan
Eglwysbach
Pen-y-fyddin
Wenallt
A548
Caerhun
Llyn Syberi
Llyn Anafon
Llanbedr-y-cennin
Pentrer Felin
Hafotty Bennent
Gell
Drum
Pen-y-Gader
Pentre Isaf
Tre-pys-llygod
Llwytmor
Pen-y-Castell
Bwlch-y-gaer
Y Bedol Inn
Tal-y-bont
Celf-coch
Mwdwl Eithin
Foel Fras
River Ditu
Dolgarrog Memorial
Dolgarrog
Llangernyw
Melai
Hafodunos
B5382
Pent-newydd
Reservoir
Craig-y-Dulyn
Dulyn Reservoir
River Porth-llwyd
Pont Dolgarrog
Rhos-y-mawn
The Abbey
Bryn Glas
Wenlli
Foel Grach
Melynllyn
Llyn Eigiau Reservoir
Moel Eilio
Aqueduct
River Ddu
Roman Spa Tearooms
Vale of
Tyn-y-fford
1
2
3
4
5
6
7
8
9
10
11
12
33
34
35
36
37
38
39
40
41
42
43
44
45
46
47
48
49
50
A
F
P

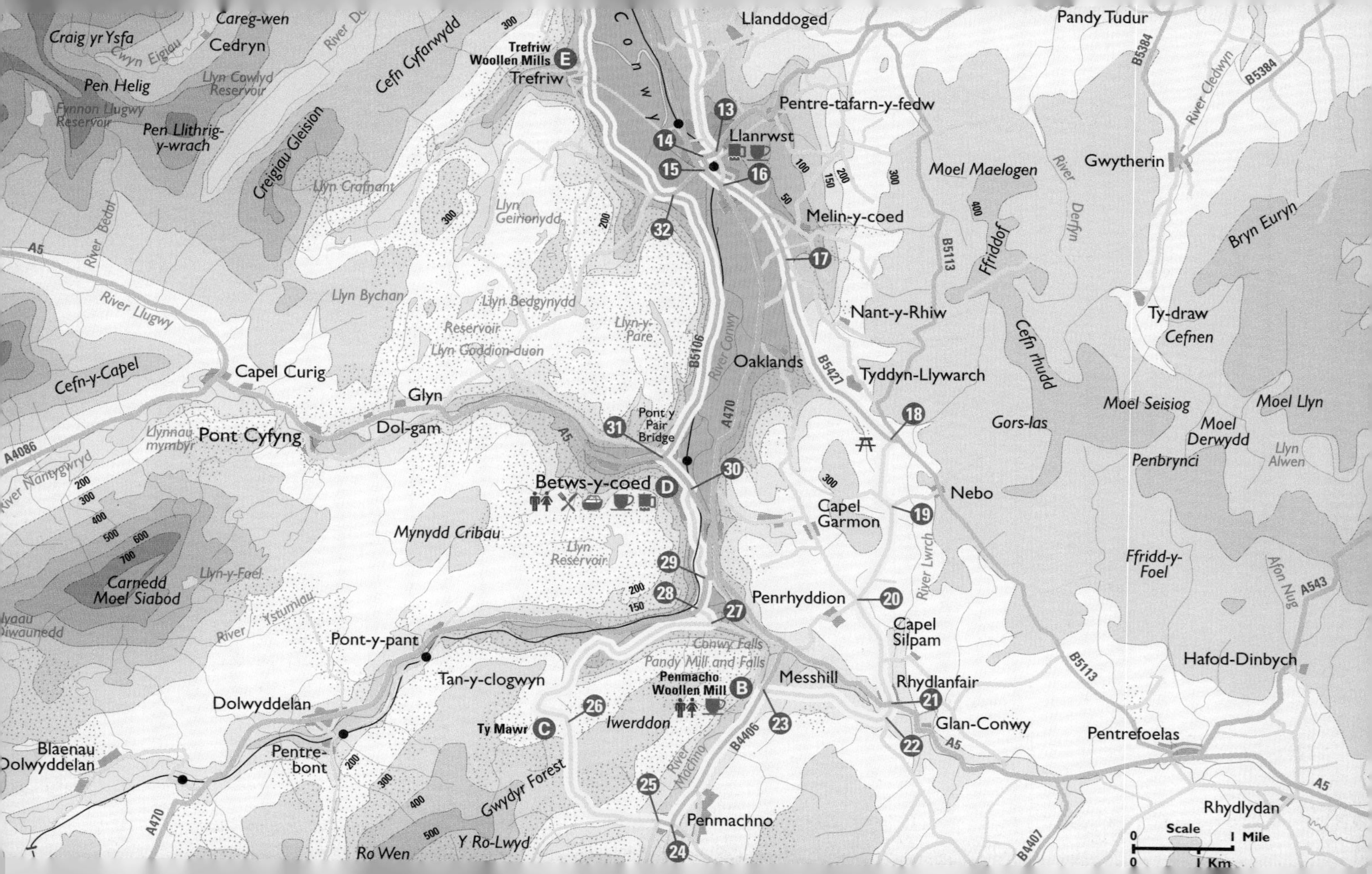

Craig yr Ysfa
Careg-wen
Cedryn
Cwyn Eigiau
Pen Helig
Llyn Cowlyd Reservoir
Fynnon Llugwy Reservoir
Pen Llithrig-y-wrach
Creigiau Gleision
Cefn Cyfarwydd
River Dulyn
300
Trefriw Woollen Mills
E
Trefriw
Conwy
Llanddoged
Pandy Tudur
B5384
River Cledwyn
B5384
13
Pentre-tafarn-y-fedw
14
Llanrwst
15
16
100
150
200
300
50
Moel Maelogen
Gwytherin
River Derfyn
Llyn Crafnant
Llyn Geirionydd
300
200
32
Melin-y-coed
400
B5113
Ffriddof
Bryn Euryn
A5
River Bedol
17
River Llugwy
Llyn Bychan
Llyn Bedgynydd
Reservoir
Llyn Goddion-duon
Llyn-y-Parc
Nant-y-Rhiw
Ty-draw
Cefnen
Cefn rhudd
Cefn-y-Capel
Capel Curig
B5106
River Conwy
Oaklands
B5427
Tyddyn-Llywarch
Glyn
Moel Seisiog
Moel Llyn
A470
18
Gors-las
Moel Derwydd
Penbrynci
Llyn Alwen
Llynnau mymbyr
Pont Cyfyng
Dol-gam
A5
31
Pont y Pair Bridge
A4086
River Nantygwryd
30
Betws-y-coed
D
Nebo
300
200
400
500
600
700
Capel Garmon
19
Mynydd Cribau
Llyn Reservoir
29
Ffridd-y-Foel
Afon Nug
A543
Llyn-y-Foel
Carnedd Moel Siabod
200
28
150
River Lwrch
Penrhyddion
20
27
Afon Cwmnaunedd
River Ystumiau
Pont-y-pant
Conwy Falls
Pandy Mill and Falls
Capel Silpam
Messhill
B5113
Hafod-Dinbych
Tan-y-clogwyn
Penmacho Woollen Mill
B
Rhydlanfair
21
Dolwyddelan
26
Ty Mawr
C
Iwerddon
23
Glan-Conwy
Pentrefoelas
B4406
22
A5
Blaenau Dolwyddelan
Pentre-bont
200
River Machno
300
25
A5
Rhydlydan
A470
400
Gwydyr Forest
Penmachno
500
Y Ro-Lwyd
Ro Wen
24
B4407
Scale
0
1 Mile
0
1 Km

Route description

Note that CW = Cycleway.

TR out of car park, no SP.

1 TL, SP Trefriw, and climb.

2 TL by Groes Inn car park, no SP. ***4km (2.5 miles)***

3 TL at TJ and cross River Conwy, no SP.

4 SO uphill at slightly offset XR. Follow SP CW for long climb.

5 TR, no SP.

6 TL and follow SP CW, soon passing lake on RHS. ***10km (6 miles)***

7 Pass under power lines and immediately keep R. Descend steeply.

8 TL following SP CW.

9 TR at TJ and follow SP CW.

10 SO, SP Llanrwst. ***15km (9.5 miles)***

11 TR, SP Llanrwst.

12 Keep L, SP Llanrwst.

13 TR at XR, SP Town Centre. ***19km (12 miles)***

14 TL into Watling Street (there is a good café on RHS).

15 TL at TJ onto A470, SP Betwys-y-coed. (TR here and immediately TL over bridge for another café – to shorten the route, continue and TR at direction 32.)

16 TL and immediately TR, SP Nebo. This is the start of a 5.5km (3.5 mile) climb.

17 Keep R, SP Nebo. Follow SP CW.

18 TR, no SP (this is a good picnic spot). ***25.5km (16 miles)***

19 Continue, following SP CW.

20 TL at TJ, SP A5.

21 SO WITH CARE at XR across A5. Immediately cross hump backed bridge – DO NOT FOLLOW blue SP CW down A5. ***30.5km (19 miles)***

22 TR, no SP. Continue to follow SP CW.

23 TL at XR opposite Penmachno Woollen Mill.

24 TR in Penmachno (by Eagles Hotel), SP Ty Mawr. ***36km (22.5 miles)***

25 Keep R up hill for 1.5km (1 mile), SP Ty Mawr. From top continue for steep and twisty descent on poor surface.

26 Pass Ty Mawr on LHS (40km/25 miles). As road descends towards Betwys the surface gets worse and becomes very steep in places. It is divided into sections by five gates and there might also be sheep on the road – beware!

27 TL at TJ, no SP.

28 TR at TJ, SP Betwys/A470.

29 Continue SO when A470 goes sharp R. Follow SP CW into Betwys-y-coed.

30 TL at TJ. ***46.5km (29 miles)***

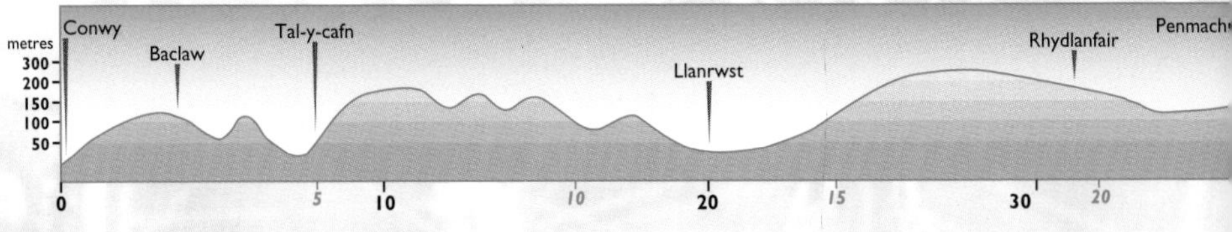

31 TR across Pont y Pair bridge, SP Trefriw/Llanrwst – TAKE CARE, bridge is narrow and often crowded with pedestrians.

32 TL at TJ, SP Trefriw.

33 Pass Roman Spa tearooms on LHS (57km/35.5 miles). Continue through Dolgarrog.

34 Just through Dolgarrog is the memorial to the dam disaster. Find it on a boulder next to SP Road Narrows. Continue into Tal-y-bont.

35 TL by Y Bedol Inn, SP Llanbedr-y-cennin, for more climbing.

36 TR by Bull pub, no SP.

37 Keep R downhill and follow SP CW.

38 TL at TJ, no SP. Continue and follow SP CW.

39 Cross bridge and keep R, no SP.

40 TR at TJ, no SP.

41 TL, SP Henryd. ***66.5km (41.5 miles)***

42 Keep R and follow SP CW.

43 TR at TJ, SP Henryd. Continue into Henryd.

44 TL by school, no SP, and follow SP CW.

45 TL and follow SP CW.

46 TR at XR, no SP. ***70km (43.5 miles)***

47 TL at TJ, no SP.

48 TR at TJ and go through town wall.

49 TL at XR and go through town wall. Immediately TR into Town Ditch Road (town walls on RHS).

50 TL (effectively SO as main road bends sharp R) into Lower Gate Street. Pass through town wall again, onto Conwy Quay. Continue along quay to main road in front of castle. Dismount, cross road and TR to mini round-about. Remount. If you started from Conwy or Llandudno retrace route to station to complete the route.

Otherwise, TL at roundabout, with castle on LHS. Go through walls for last time and continue to car park and the end of the ride.

74km (46 miles)

Food and drink

This ride is extremely strenuous and you should carry plenty of drink and high energy food to sustain you. There are plenty of catering establishments along the route: Conwy has several cafés and hotels, and ice cream is sold on the quay (passed at the end of the ride). There is also plenty of choice in Llanrwst and Betwys-y-coed and refreshments are available at many of the places of interest.

Roman Spa Tearooms, near Trefriw
A good place for afternoon tea.

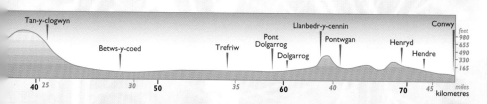

Tan-y-clogwyn | Betws-y-coed | Trefriw | Pont Dolgarrog | Dolgarrog | Llanbedr-y-cennin | Pontwgan | Henryd | Hendre | Conwy

feet: 980, 655, 490, 330, 165

miles: 25, 30, 35, 40, 45

kilometres: 40, 50, 60, 70

Route **22**

CORWEN AND BWLCH-Y-GROES

Route information

Distance 90km (56 miles)

Grade Strenuous

Terrain Undulating minor roads except for two short stretches on A road by Corwen and Bala. There are long climbs and descents to and from Lake Vyrnwy.

Time to allow 5–8 hours.

Getting there by car Corwen is on the A5 close to the junction with the A494. There is free long-term parking in the town.

Getting there by train There is no practical rail access to this ride.

Starting from Corwen, the route heads west along the picturesque Upper Dee Valley to the market town of Bala. On alongside Bala Lake, the largest natural lake in Wales for a long steep climb up Cwm Cynllwyd to Bwlch y Groes (spectacular views). A descent takes you to Lake Vyrnwy. After crossing the dam, the route runs beside the reservoir before climbing out of the valley, descending Cwm Hirnant and returning to Corwen.

Places of interest along the route

A Corwen

A market town and once the headquarters of Owain Glyndwr, the medieval freedom fighter who fought against the English. **Corwen Manor**, located in the old workhouse, comprises a craft, candle and jewellery shop, crazy golf, butterfly house and café. Open January to March, Friday–Monday 0999–1700; April, May, November and December, daily except Wednesday; June to October, daily. Admission free. Telephone (01490) 413196. Medieval **Llangar Church** is in an idyllic setting, overlooking the confluence of the Dee and Alwen rivers. The church contains many ancient features including 15th-century wall paintings. Cadw (Welsh Historic Monuments) property. Open May to September, Tuesday–Saturday and Bank Holidays (by arrangement) 1400–1500. Charge. Telephone Rug Chapel for more information. Nearby (1.5km/1 mile north west from Corwen on the A494) is **Rug Chapel**. This is a little-altered private 17th-century chapel containing a richly carved and painted roof, altar, pews and gallery. Cadw property. Open May to September, Tuesday–Saturday and Bank Holiday Mondays 1000–1400 and 1500–1700. Charge. Telephone (01490) 412025.

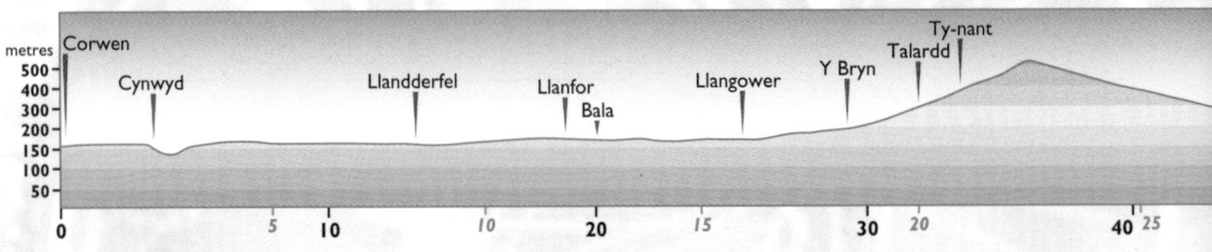

B Bala Lake

Bala Lake (Llyn Tegid) is Wales' largest natural lake and home to a wide range of wildlife. The Bala Lake Railway is a narrow gauge line that runs along the eastern shore of the lake, between Bala and Llanuwchllyn. See route 3 for more information.

C Bwlch y Groes

The viewpoint here (at 546m/1800 feet) offers spectacular views of the surrounding mountain scenery, with Arrenig Fawr to the north, the Arran Range to the west and Snowdonia in the distance.

D Lake Vyrnwy, near Dolanog

A man-made lake created in the 1880s to supply Liverpool with water. See route 9 for more information.

Also passed en route is an ancient circle of standing stones.

Route description

TL out of Corwen car park into Green Lane. TR at TJ onto A5 and continue on A5 out of town.

1 TL before crossing river, SP Cynwyd/Llandrillo/B4401. Continue into Cynwyd, passing Llangar Church.

2 TR opposite Blue Lion in Cynwyd, no SP (4km/2.5 miles). Continue to cross river and immediately:

3 TL, no SP. Continue on this road, following River Dee and passing standing stones. Arrive at Llandderfel.

4 Cycle into village and TL at TJ, no SP.

8.5km (5 miles)

5 TR at TJ by war memorial, SP Bala 4 miles.

6 TL at TJ onto A494, SP Bala (11km/7 miles), and continue into Bala.

7 To visit Loch Café, TR (opposite Royal White Lion Hotel). Otherwise, TL into Tegid Street, no SP.

8 TR at TJ onto B4391, no SP.

20km (12.5 miles)

9 TR , SP Llangower/Bala Lake Railway/B4403. Continue on this road along the shore of Bala Lake.

10 TL, SP Dinas Mawddwy (28km/17.5 miles), and climb Cwm Cynllwyd to Bwlch y Groes and view point.

11 TL sharply, SP Lake Vyrnwy (36km/22.5 miles). Continue to lake.

12 TR at TJ, SP Visitor Centre (42km/26 miles), and continue alongside lake to dam.

13 Arrive dam (49km/30.5 miles). To visit Vyrnwy village, tearooms and Tourist Information Centre continue SO.

Otherwise, TL across dam, then TL at TJ, no SP. Continue alongside lake.

14 TR, SP Rhos-y-gwalia/Bala (57.5km/35.5 miles). Continue on this road for climb and descent to Rhos-y-gwalia.

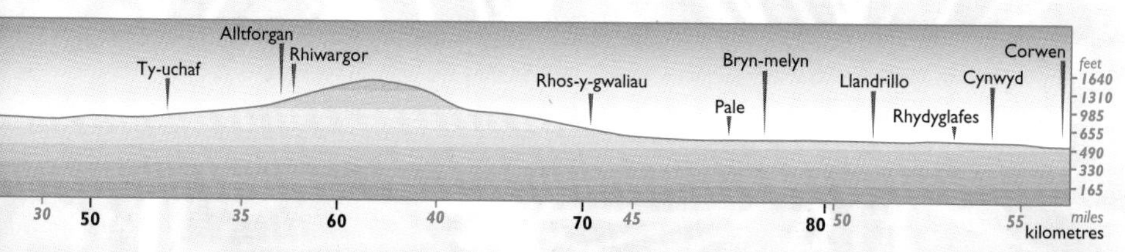

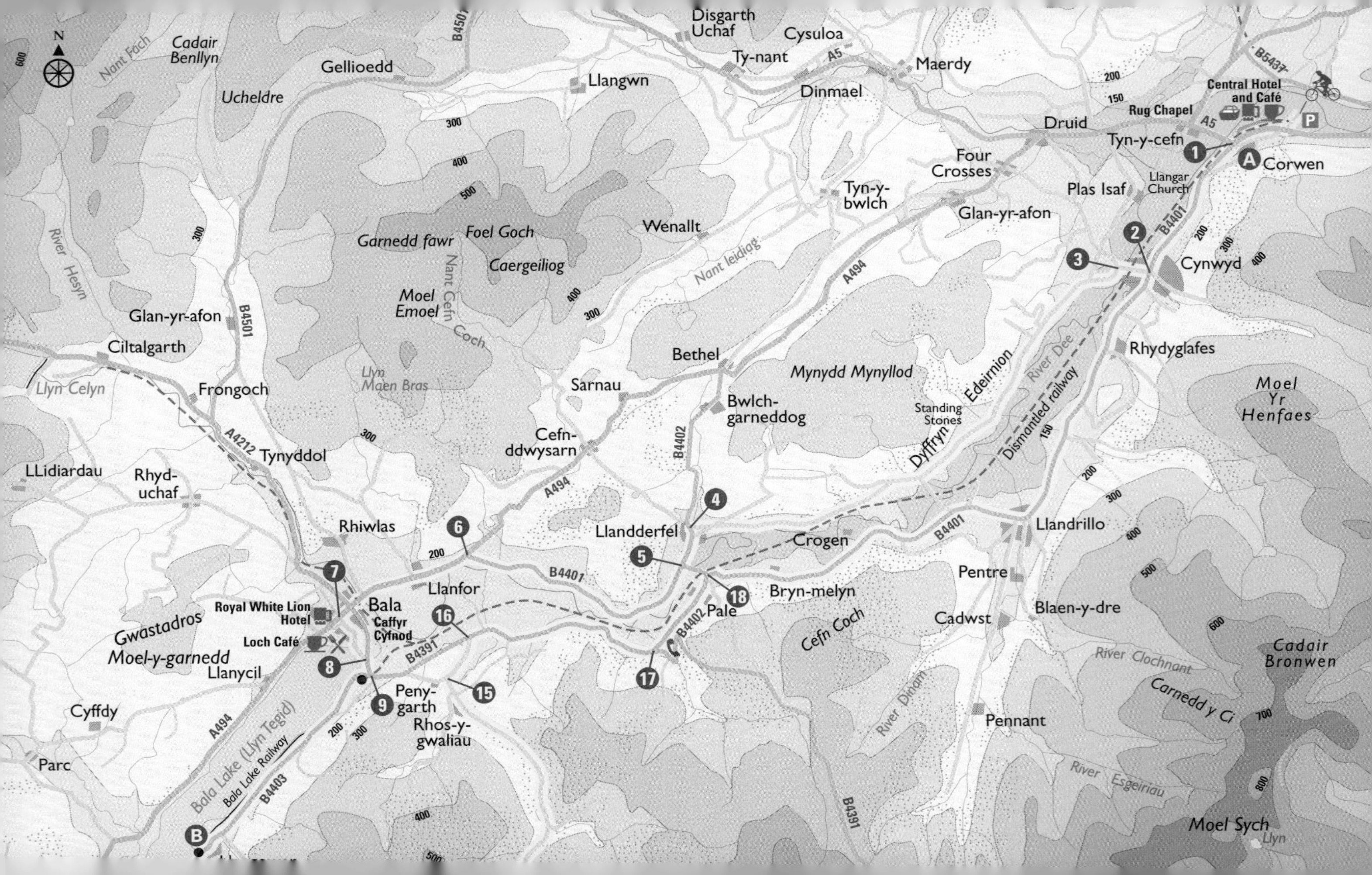

N
Cadair Benllyn
Nant Fach
Gellioedd
Ucheldre
Disgarth Uchaf
Cysuloa
Ty-nant
A5
Maerdy
Llangwn
Dinmael
B4501
B5437
Central Hotel and Café
Rug Chapel
Druid
Tyn-y-cefn
Corwen
Four Crosses
Plas Isaf
Llangar Church
Tyn-y-bwlch
Glan-yr-afon
Wenallt
Nant Ieidiog
A494
B4401
Cynwyd
Garnedd fawr
Foel Goch
Caergeiliog
Nant Cefn Coch
Moel Emoel
River Hesyn
Glan-yr-afon
Ciltalgarth
Llyn Celyn
Frongoch
Llyn Maen Bras
Bethel
Sarnau
Mynydd Mynyllod
Standing Stones
Dyffryn Edeirnion
River Dee
Dismantled railway
Rhydyglafes
Moel Yr Henfaes
Bwlch-garneddog
B4402
Cefn-ddwysarn
A4212
Tynyddol
LLidiardau
Rhyd-uchaf
Rhiwlas
Llandderfel
Crogen
Llandrillo
Pentre
Bryn-melyn
Pale
Blaen-y-dre
Cadwst
Cefn Coch
Llanfor
Bala
Royal White Lion Hotel
Caffyr Cyfnod
Loch Café
Gwastadros
Moel-y-garnedd
Llanycil
B4391
Peny-garth
Rhos-y-gwaliau
Cyffdy
Parc
Bala Lake (Llyn Tegid)
Bala Lake Railway
B4403
River Clochnant
Cadair Bronwen
Carnedd y Ci
River Dinam
Pennant
River Esgeiriau
Moel Sych
Llyn

Llanuwchllyn
Pentre-piod
Y Bryn
Rhyd-wen
Nant Rhyd-wen
Afon Fechan
Foel Figenau
Cwm Cynllwyd
Afon Twrch
Talardd
Ty-nant
Moel Ddu
L.Llymbren
Cwm Groes
Faol y Geifr
Cwm Hirnant
Pen y Boncyn Trefeilw
Cyrniau Nod
Craig Wen
Careg Wen
Trum y Fawnog
Afon Yn-y-Groes
Milltir Gerrig
Blaen Glaswen
Post Gwyn
Tan-y-pistyll
Craig Mwn
Afon Rhaeadr
Y Clogydd
Afon Rhiweirth
B4391
Pencraig
Glan-hafon
Pennant Melangell
Afon Tanad
Llangynog
Pentre
Moel Dimoel
Llyn-y-Mynydd
Penybontfawr
Bwlch-y-Main
Craig ddu
Ffordd Gefu
B4396
Cwm Hirnant
Hirnant
Bwlch Sych
Afon y Dolau-gwynion
Afon Cedig
Cedig
River Iddew
Rhiwargor
Alltforgan
Moel-cerrig-duon
Bwlch y Groes
Foel Rudd
Allt-y-Eryr
Allt-y-Grib
Moel y Bryn
B4393
Eunant Fawr
Craiglyn Dyfi
Craig Ty-naint
Bryn Mawr
Lake Vyrnwy
Ty-uchaf
Llaethnant
Ogof Ddu
Afon Dyfi
Hirddu Fawr
Mynydd St John or Cefn Tre-ysbyty
Coed Cochion
Pumryd
Afon Pumryd
Llanymawddwy
Cwm Terwyn
Maenaidd
Tap Mawr
Bryn Mawr
Blaen Cownwy
Hen Gerrig
Afon Twrch
Afon Cownwy
Penisarcwn
Pen y Ffridd-Cownwy
Plantiau
Llechwedd Du
Foel yr Hydd
Llanwddyn
Abertridwr
Pen y Bylchau
Mandys Café
Craig Garth bwlch
Ddol Cownwy
Yr Allt Boeth
Boncyn Celyn
B4395
Llanfihangel-yng-Ngwynfa
Scale
0 1 Mile
0 1 Km
10
11
12
13
14
C
D

15 TR, no SP.

16 TR at TJ onto B4391, no SP.

17 TL by telephone box, SP Corwen B4402 (B4401).

18 TR at TJ, SP Corwen B4401. Continue through Llandrillo and Cynwyd and TR at TJ onto A5. Follow A5 into Corwen to complete the route. ***90km (56 miles)***

Food and drink

Corwen has a hotel and café and refreshments are available at Corwen Manor, Bala and Lake Vyrnwy.

Loch Café, Bala
Lakeside tearoom and restaurant.

Royal White Lion Hotel, Bala
Pub, hotel and restaurant in the centre of town.

Mandy's Café, Lake Vyrnwy
Snacks and light lunches.

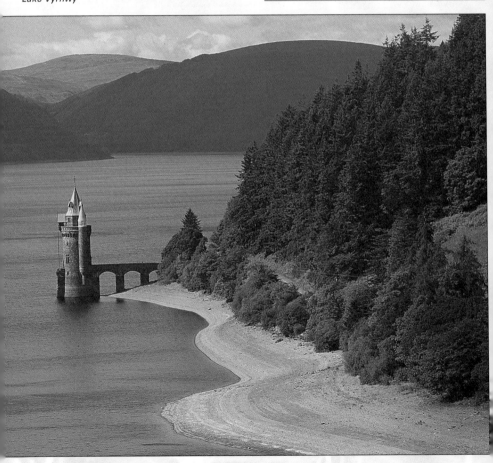

Lake Vyrnwy

Route **23**

OSWESTRY AND THE DEVIL'S CHAIR

Route information

Distance 94km (58.5 miles)

Grade Moderate

Terrain The route covers a rural area of Shropshire and the Welsh borderlands, mostly along narrow, twisting lanes. There are occasional stretches of main road but these are usually not too busy.

Time to allow 7–8 hours.

Getting there by car Oswestry is off the A483. Take the B5069 into town. Soon after entering one way system, TL (opposite Somerfield on RHS) into car park (pay and display but free on Sundays. Note: there is an overhead height restriction here but bicycles on most roof racks will be OK – check first!

Getting there by train The nearest station is Gobowen some 4km (2.5 miles) from Oswestry. Telephone (0345) 484950 for travel information. TL out of station and take the B5069 into Oswestry. Continue to car park (start of the route) as above.

From Oswestry on the Welsh border across the flat ground of the River Severn valley before rising steadily into the north end of the Shropshire hills. From the summit of the Stiperstones Ridge there is a long, steady descent back to the Severn Valley and a flat ride back to Oswestry. An optional short distance of off-road will shorten the ride slightly.

Places of interest along the route

A Oswestry

On the Welsh/English border, the ancient town of Oswestry grew up around King Oswald's Well. At varying times through history Oswestry has been both Welsh and English. The town trail is a good way to explore – leaflets are available from the Tourist Information Centre. The town's market is one of the country's busiest, with over 120 stalls. Markets are held all year on Wednesdays and on Saturdays during the summer. Oswestry was the headquarters of the old Cambrian Railway and at the centre of the of the rail network serving north and mid-Wales. The **Cambrian Museum of Transport** describes the railway's history and has a collection of memorabilia and artefacts, and a small number of bicycles and mopeds. Locomotives are regularly steamed up. Open all year: summer 1000–16500; winter 1000–1500. Nominal charge. Telephone (01691) 671749. Just north of the town is **Old Oswestry Hillfort**, one of the best examples of an Iron Age hill fort, with massive earthwork ramparts. There are spectacular views from the top. **Oswestry Heritage Centre** contains the Tourist Information Centre and exhibitions describing everyday life in days gone by. Also craft shop and café. Open all year, Monday–Saturday 0930–1700. Tele- phone (01691) 662753

B Melverly Church

This small, timber-framed building on the banks of the River Severn is the oldest church in Shropshire, dating from 1406. Telephone Oswestry Tourist Information Centre for further information.

N
Lledrod
Llawnt
Pant-glas
Brogyntyn
To Gobowen Station
Park Hall Camp
Oswestry
Whittington
Babbinswood
Hordley
Tetchill Moor
Lower Hordley
Rednal
Haughton
Grimpo
West Felton
Wykey
Eardiston
Cockshutt
Stanwardine in the Wood
Bagley
Weston Lullingfields
Stanwardine in the Fields
Pikes End Moss
Crose Mere
Sweat Mere
Wolverley
Newtown
English Frankton
Loppington
Noneley
Burlton
Myddle
Eyton
Croesau Bach
Morda
Llyn Rhuddwyn
River Morda
Mynydd Myfyr
Trefonen
Treflach
Nantmawr
Llynclys
Porth-y-waen
Pen-y-bont
Llanyblodwel
Ball
Maesbury Marsh
Montgomery Canal
Weirbrook
Woolston
Morton
Sandford
Crickheath
Pant
Knockin
Maesbrook
Kinnerley
Dovaston
Ruyton-XI-Towns
Newtown
Baschurch
Prescott
Walford
Old Woods
Hopton
Kynaston
Nesscliffe
Llanymynech
Llansantffraid-ym-Mechain
Dismantled railway
River Vyrnwy
Waen
Llandysilio
Domgay
Four Crosses
Haughton
Crosslanes
Edgerley
Kinton
Wilcott
Great Ness
Yeaton
Walford Heath
Grafton
Leaton
Fitz
The Isle
Broomfields
Felton Butler
Melverley Green
Melverley
River Severn
Ensdon
Forton
Rosehill
Bicton
Deuddwr
Llandrinio
R. Vyrnwy
Melverley Church
Tontine Inn
Sarnau
Arddlin
Crewgreen
Criggion
Coedway
Fir Tree Inn
Old Hand & Diamond
Alberbury
Shrawardine
Montford Bridge
Montford
Preston Montford
Eyton
Breidden Hill
Geufford
River Perry
lansilin
B4579
B4580
B5009
A495
B5069
A483
A5
B4396
B4398
B4397
B4393
B5067
B4380
A528
B5063
B4392

SHREWSBURY
Stanford
Windmill
Moel y Golfa
Wollaston
Rowton
Cardeston
Shoot Hill
Dismantled railway
Pool Quay
Middletown
Trewern
Guilsfield
Groes-lwyd
Halfway House
Ford Heath
Nox
Cruckton
Great Hanwood
Rea Brook
Stretton Heath
Yockleton
Cruckmeole
Hook-a-gate
Vennington
Frochas
Buttington
Westbury
Stoney Stretton
Edge
Hinton
Bayston Hill
Annscroft
WALES
ENGLAND
Lower Wallop
Farley
Great Lyth
Lythbank
Welshpool (Y Trallwyng)
Hope
Long Mountain
Rowley
Aston Rogers
Westley
Asterley
Railway Inn
Plealey
Exfords Green
Aston Pigott
Pontesbury
Pontesford
Longden
Plough
Leighton
Minsterley
Oaks
Longden Common
Short Cross
Brockton
Worthen
Ploxgreen
Stapleton
Binweston
Llwynderw
Fron
Trelystan
Leigh
Wrentnall
Habberley
Wagbeach
Dorrington
Marton
Marton Pool
Pulverbatch
Church Pulverbatch
Kingswood
Wilmington
Betton
Hope
Snailbeach
Stiperstones Ridge
Crowsnest
Cothercott
Scale
0
1 Mile
0
1 Km
Stockton
Meadowtown
Forden
Stiperstones Inn
Wotherton
Woodmoor
Rorrington
Underhill Hall
Gravels
Hope Valley
Longmor Park
Walcot
Pennerley
Devils Chair
Picklescott
River Severn
River Camlad
Heightley
Stiperstones
Shelve
Winsbury
Chirbury
Lower Ridge
Mitchell's Fold
Stapeley Hill
Betchcott
Woolstaston
Betchcott Hill
The Bog
Ratlinghope Hill
Dudston
The Marsh
Darnford
Womerton
Lower Lane
Priestweston
Stedment
Ratlinghope
High Park
Montgomery
Corndon Hill
Nind
Black Rhadley Hill
Kinnerton
Bridges
Wild Moor
Haddon Hill
All Stretton
Montgomery Canal
A458
A483
A490
A488
A5
A49
B4386
B4387
B4388
B4499

C Breidden Hill

The roue passes close to the Breidden Hill and Rodney's Pillar, a monument erected by the Gentlemen of Montgomeryshire to Admiral Rodney, the victor against the French at the 1782 Battle of Saintes in the West Indies.

D Stiperstones Ridge

The ridge and the surrounding district was an important mining area during the 19th century. On the RHS of the road on the approach to Snailbeach you will see details of a heritage trail around the old Snailbeach mine. The Stiperstones are a National Nature Reserve and cycling on the paths is strictly forbidden. Apart from that, the paths soon become extremely rocky making walking difficult and cycling impossible. If you decide to go to the summit of the ridge, secure your bike to the car park fence and walk. The views from the ridge are stunning and the small effort of walking to the top is worthwhile.

E Devil's Chair

The Devil's Chair is part of the Stiperstones and the rocky outcrops are similar to Dartmoor's tors. Local legend has it that the Devil has never been seen in his chair as he only occupies it when the cloud is down over the ridge!

Route description

TL out of car park, no SP. Pass Cambrian Museum of Transport on LHS.

1 TL at XR into Leg Street. Soon after arrive at TJ (with superstore entrance) and continue SO.

2 TR, SP Maesbury Road Industrial Estate.

3 TR, SP Welshpool, and immediately TL, SP Maesbury/Knockin. TAKE CARE at this busy junction.

4 TR into Back Lane, SP Morton.

5 TR at TJ into Morton Lane (5km/3 miles). Follow SP for Morton and then for Llynclys.

6 SO at XR, SP Llwyntidmon. SO at next XR, SP Llwyntidmon, and continue on this road.

7 TL at TJ, SP Maesbrook/Knockin (11km/7 miles). Then TR, SP Dyffryd.

8 TR at TJ, SP Melverley.

9 Keep L, SP Melverley Church.

16.5km (10.5 miles)

10 To visit Melverley Church, TR by Tontine Inn and continue along lane for approximately 200m. After visit, retrace route to inn and TR to continue route.

Otherwise, continue SO, with Tontine Inn on RHS.

11 Cross River Severn. On RHS, about 300m upstream, you will see the confluence of the Rivers Vyrnwy and Severn.

12 TL at TJ, SP Shrewsbury (20km/12.5 miles). Pass Fir Tree Inn on RHS, then Old Hand and Diamond Inn on RHS.

13 TR, SP Halfway House for a moderate climb.

14 Pass Hole Farm on LHS (25km/15.5 miles).

15 Follow SP Halfway House/Westbury.

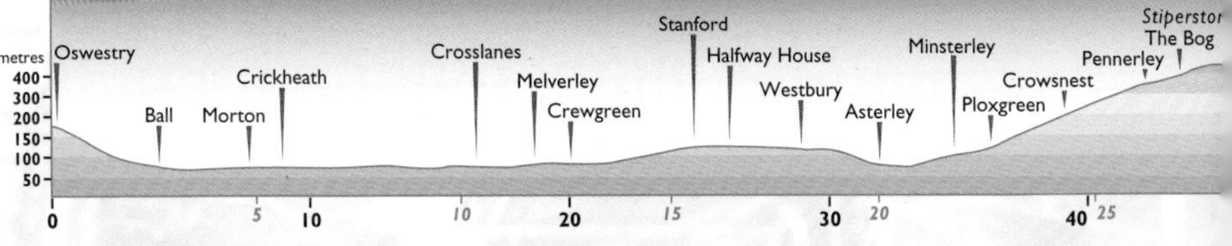

16 SO at XR onto B4387, SP Westbury/ Minsterley.

17 SO at XR, SP Asterley/Pontesbury (29km/18 miles)

18 TR at TJ, SP Minsterley.

19 TL at TJ, SP Minsterley.

20 TL at roundabout, SP Shrewsbury/ Bishop's Castle. At next roundabout, TR, SP Bishop's Castle (Bridge Hotel is on LHS as you enter this roundabout). ***35km (21.5 miles)***

21 TL, SP Snailbeach/Stiperstones. The climbing becomes harder and continues for approximately 9km (5.5 miles).

22 Continue up hill, passing Snailbeach Mine on LHS.

23 Continue climb and pass Stiperstones Inn on LHS (40.5km/25 miles). Continue and follow SP The Bog.

24 Arrive The Bog car park on RHS. Keep L, SP Bridges/Wentnor, for steep climb.

25 Arrive SP Ice and Snow in Winter and TL.

26 TL into car park (immediately before cattle grid – 45.5km/28.5 miles). If you want to walk up the Tors, leave your bike secured in car park and take path up hill (cycling forbidden). The Devil's Chair is, naturally enough, the furthest outcrop and the return walk will probably take about an hour. If you don't want to walk as far as that, at least get to the top of the ridge for superb all round views (should take around 35/40 minutes). Be warned – the ground becomes rocky and modern cycling shoes are not suitable footwear for this terrain, but you should be able to manage with care.

For the optional off-road section, take bridleway which starts from far end of this car park. Follow it along hillside below a clear felled wood to a gate. The ground here is pretty rough and wet but is rideable with care. After gate the track becomes relatively indistinct, but keep to top edge of field and it soon becomes obvious again. Arrive at TJ and TR downhill past Hollies Farm, where you rejoin tarmac road. Continue downhill to TJ where TL and rejoin route at direction 29.

To stay on-road, TL out of car park and immediately cross cattle grid for long, steep descent along an unfenced road (which may be obstructed by cattle or sheep – take care!) Cattle grids are frequent for the next few km.

27 Easy to miss – TL sharply (on steep descent, next to farm buildings on RHS by yellow grit bin), no SP.

28 Continue SO (49.5km/31 miles) and up moderate hill, after which route goes downhill for a 7km (4.5 mile) stretch.

29 TL at TJ, no SP. Continue into Habberley.

30 TL at TJ by St Mary's Church (55.5km/ 34.5 miles). Then keep R, SP Pontesbury. Continue and pass Plough pub on RHS.

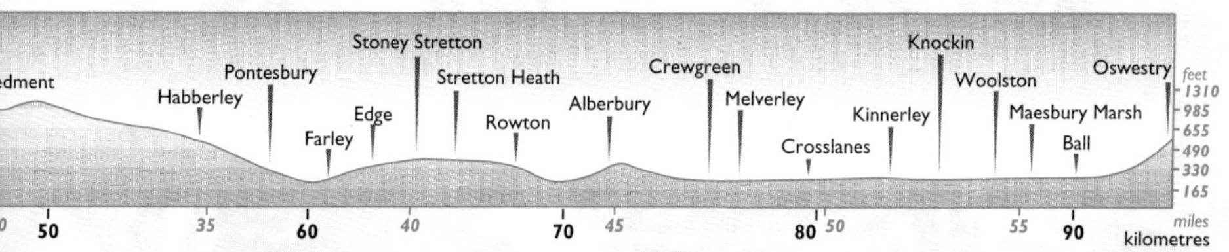

31 TL at TJ, no SP. Then SO at XR by Railway Inn, SP Farley.

32 TR at TJ, SP Edge. ***61km (38 miles)***

33 TL at TJ, no SP. Then SO at XR, SP Stretton Heath/Rowton.

34 Keep L, SP Stoney Stretton.

35 SO at XR, SP Stretton Heath/Rowton. ***64.5km (40 miles)***

36 TR at TJ onto A458, SP Shrewsbury. Continue and pass Windmill Pub on LHS.

37 TL, SP Alberbury/Four Crosses.

38 TL at TJ, SP Four Crosses (71.5km/ 44.5 miles). Continue, retracing earlier route for few km.

39 TR, SP Melverley. ***75.5km (47 miles)***

40 Keep L, SP Maesbrook.

41 Keep R by post box, SP Maesbrook.

42 TR, SP Argoed/Kinnerley. Then follow SP Kinnerley/Knockin. ***82km (51miles)***

43 TL at TJ, SP Knockin. Then TL, SP Knockin/Oswestry.

44 TL at TJ onto B4396 , SP Llynclys/ Oswestry.

45 TR, SP Maesbury/Oswestry (85.5km/ 53 miles). Continue towards Oswestry.

46 TR at TJ then immediately TL, SP Maesbury Road Industrial Estate ***91.5km (57 miles)***

47 TL at TJ, no SP, but soon follow SP Town Centre. SO at superstore.

48 SO at XR into one way system and keep to RHS to return to car park and end of ride. ***94km (58.5 miles)***

If returning to Gobowen station, keep to LHS. When two way traffic system restarts, bear left and retrace route back to station.

Food and drink

There is plenty of choice in Oswestry, but most places close on Sundays. Because of the rural nature of the countryside, many of the pubs en route only open in the evenings, except at weekends or during the summer holidays. You should carry drinks and snacks to sustain you during the ride.

Stiperstones Inn, Stiperstones
The one certainty for good food and superb views on any day of the year, at any time. Since this is almost the halfway point in the ride and is in the middle of a long climb up from the Severn Valley, it is also highly convenient.

Old Hand and Diamond Inn, Coedway
A suitable mid-morning and afternoon stop. Telephone to confirm opening times on (01743) 884379.

Windmill, Rowton
Often closed at midday on weekdays but may open by request if given prior notice. Telephone (01743) 884234.

Tontine Inn, near Melverly Church
Open daily, Monday–Saturday 1100–2300, Sunday 1200–2300. If cycling in a large group and planning to use the pub, please telephone in advance on (01691) 682258.

Route **24**

MENAI BRIDGE TO BEDDGELERT

Route information

Distance 95km (59 miles)

Grade Strenuous

Terrain Traffic-free cycleway, quiet lanes and A roads (on which traffic is quite light). There are some climbs, for which low gears will be necessary.

Time to allow 5–6 hours.

Getting there by car Coed Cyrnol is just on the north side of the Menai Suspension bridge on Anglesey. Take the A5122 from Bangor. Alternatively use the A5, go over Britannia Bridge and take first exit, SP Menai Bridge. There is a car park in Coed Cyrnol (follow SP Car Park).

Getting there by train The nearest stations are at Bangor and Llanfairpwll (3km/2 miles) from the start of the route. Telephone (0345) 484950 for travel information. To start the route from Bangor station, SO at traffic lights, down hill and join route at direction 4. From Llanfairpwll station, TR out of station, TL onto A4080 and follow SP Menai Bridge.

From Coed Cyrnol on Anglesey, the route crosses Thomas Telford's magnificent Menai suspension bridge, heading for Bangor. Then on quiet roads for a climb up the Nant Ffrancon pass and on to Capel Curig. The route then passes through Snowdonia with superb views of the mountains. After a fast descent from Pen-y-Gwryd to Llyn Gwynant and Beddgelert, the road climbs to Rhyd-Ddu and on to the top of Drws-y-Coed. Another fast descent takes you to Nantlle and Penygroes before following quiet lanes back to Caernarfon. From here the route initially follows part of the Lôn Las Menai (a pleasant cycleway and part of the National Cycle Route), until it rejoins the main road back to Menai Bridge.

Route description

TR out of car park in Coed Cyrnol.

1 SO at roundabout and continue over the Menai Bridge.

2 TL at roundabout and follow A5122, SP Bangor.

3 TL into Siliwen Road, just after SP 30MPH (4.5km/3 miles). Continue to junction by boatyard.

4 TL and continue on A5122 alongside harbour, passing Penrhyn Castle.

5 SO at roundabout, SP Betws-y-coed/A5.

6 TR at junction (before crossing Halfway Bridge), SP Tregarth.

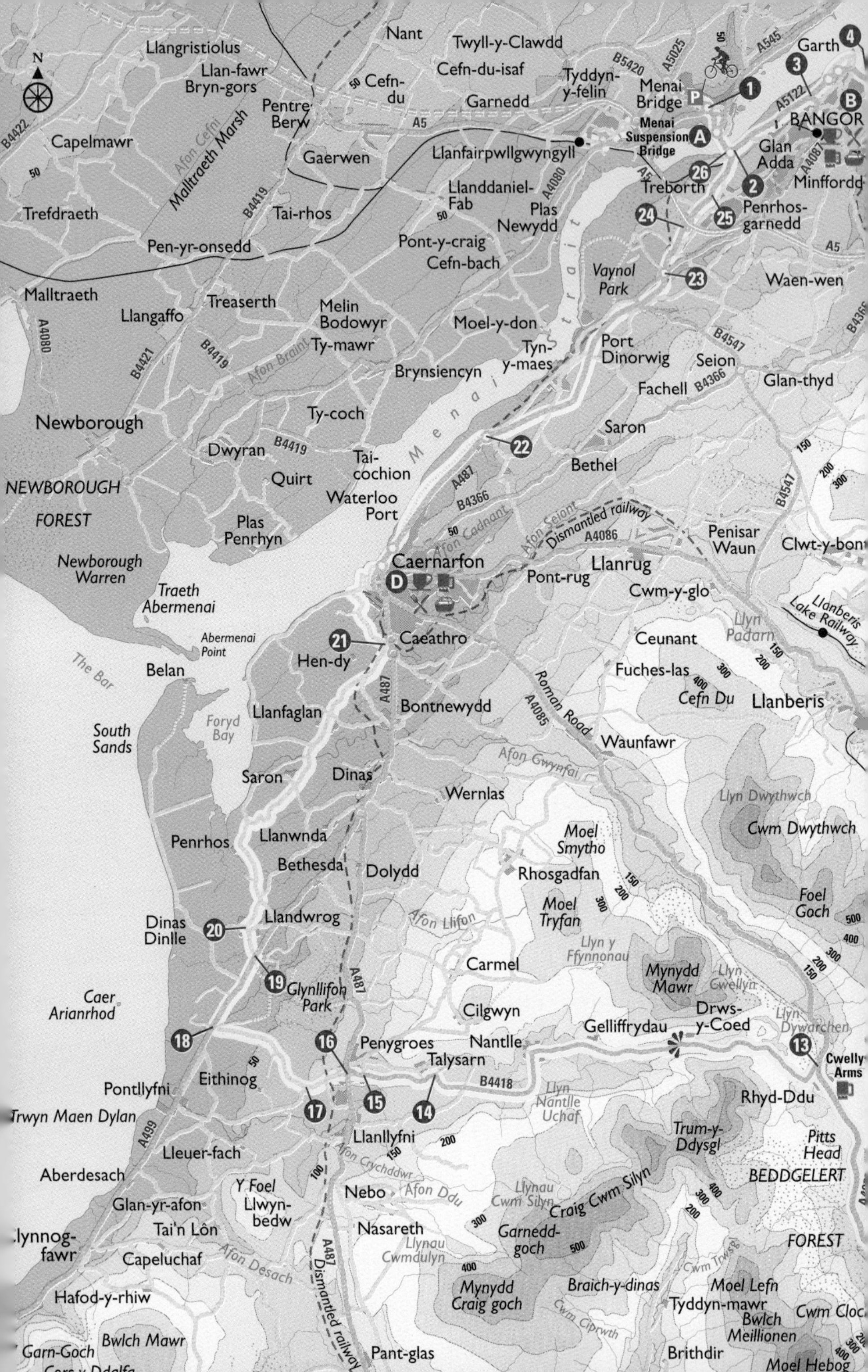
Llangristiolus
Nant
Twyll-y-Clawdd
Garth
Llan-fawr
Bryn-gors
Cefn-du
Cefn-du-isaf
Tyddyn-y-felin
Menai Bridge
BANGOR
Pentre Berw
Garnedd
Capelmawr
Malltraeth Marsh
Afon Cefni
Gaerwen
Llanfairpwllgwyngyll
Menai Suspension Bridge
Glan Adda
Minffordd
Trefdraeth
Tai-rhos
Llanddaniel-Fab
Plas Newydd
Treborth
Penrhos-garnedd
Pen-yr-onsedd
Pont-y-craig
Cefn-bach
Vaynol Park
Waen-wen
Malltraeth
Llangaffo
Treaserth
Melin Bodowyr
Moel-y-don
Ty-mawr
Afon Braint
Tyn-y-maes
Port Dinorwig
Seion
Glan-thyd
Fachell
Brynsiencyn
Menai Strait
Newborough
Ty-coch
Saron
Dwyran
Quirt
Tai-cochion
Bethel
NEWBOROUGH FOREST
Waterloo Port
Plas Penrhyn
Afon Cadnant
Afon Seiont
Dismantled railway
Penisar Waun
Clwt-y-bont
Newborough Warren
Caernarfon
Llanrug
Pont-rug
Traeth Abermenai
Cwm-y-glo
Llanberis Lake Railway
Llyn Padarn
Abermenai Point
Hen-dy
Caeathro
Ceunant
The Bar
Belan
Fuches-las
Roman Road
Cefn Du
Llanberis
Llanfaglan
Bontnewydd
Foryd Bay
South Sands
Waunfawr
Afon Gwyrfai
Saron
Dinas
Wernlas
Llyn Dwythwch
Cwm Dwythwch
Llanwnda
Moel Smytho
Penrhos
Bethesda
Dolydd
Rhosgadfan
Foel Goch
Moel Tryfan
Afon Llifon
Dinas Dinlle
Llandwrog
Llyn y Ffynnonau
Carmel
Mynydd Mawr
Llyn Cwellyn
Glynllifon Park
Caer Arianrhod
Cilgwyn
Drws-y-Coed
Gelliffrydau
Llyn Dywarchen
Nantlle
Penygroes
Talysarn
Cwelly Arms
Eithinog
Pontllyfni
Llyn Nantlle Uchaf
Rhyd-Ddu
Trwyn Maen Dylan
Trum-y-Ddysgl
Pitts Head
Llanllyfni
Lleuer-fach
Afon Crychddwr
BEDDGELERT
Aberdesach
Llynnau Cwm Silyn
Craig Cwm Silyn
Y Foel
Nebo
Afon Ddu
Glan-yr-afon
Llwyn-bedw
Tai'n Lôn
Nasareth
Garnedd-goch
Llynnog-fawr
Llynnau Cwmdulyn
FOREST
Capeluchaf
Afon Desach
Cwm Trwsgl
Moel Lefn
Mynydd Craig goch
Braich-y-dinas
Hafod-y-rhiw
Tyddyn-mawr
Bwlch Meillionen
Cwm Cloch
Cwm Ciprwth
Bwlch Mawr
Garn-Goch
Pant-glas
Brithdir
Moel Hebog
A5
A5025
A545
A5122
B5420
A4087
A4080
B4419
B4422
B4421
B4547
B4366
A487
A4086
A4085
B4418
A499
Dismantled railway

Bangor Flats
Port Penrhyn
Castle
Abergwyngregyn
Gorddinog
Garreg Fawr
Afon Ddu
Tal-y-fan
Rowen
Bwlch-y-Ddeufaen
Tai'r-meibion
A55
Llandygai
Crymlyn
Afon Rhaeadr
Yr Orsedd
Drosgl
Hafitty-gwyn
Afon Roe
Afon Anafon
Ty'n-yr-hendre
A5122
5
Tal-y-bont
Aber Falls
Llyn Anafon
Drum
Llanbedr-y-cennin
B5106
A5
6
Moel Wnion
Afon Gaai
Llwytmor
Pen-y-Castell
Bwlch-y-gaer
Glasinfryn
7
Llanllechid
Bera Mawr
Afon Goch
Tal-y-bont
Tregarth
Drosgl
Bera Bach
Foel Fras
Ditu
Waterfall
B4409
Afon Gareg-w
Dulyn
Dolgarrog
8
Rachub
Afon Ffrydlas
Tr Aryg
Pent-newydd
Reservoir
Sling
B4409
Bethesda
Craig-y-Dulyn
Dulyn Reservoir
Afon Wen
Dolgarro
9
Gerlan
Afon Caseg
Foel Grach
Porth-llwyd
Moel Eilio
Hirdir
Braichmelyn
Llyn Eigiau Reservoir
Aqueduct
Ddu
Penrhyn Slate Quarries
Ogwen Bank
Yr Elan
Gledr Ffordd
Douglas Hill
Carnedd Llywelyn
Pen-bryn-brwynog
Careg-wen
Ty'n-y-maes
Craig yr Ysfa
Cedryn
Nant Fuch
Ddu
Cefn Cyfarwydd
Carnedd-y-Filiast
Carnedd Dafydd
Fynnon Llugwy Reservoir
Pen Helig
Llyn Cowlyd Reservoir
Ty-gwyn
Nant Ffrancon
Mynydd Perfedd
Pen Llithrig-y-wrach
Creigiau Gleision
Marchlyn Mawr Res
A5
Elidyr Fawr
Llyn Crafnant
Dinorwig
Llyn Ogwen
Llyn Geirionydd
Pont Pen-y-benglog
Llyn Bedgynydd
Afon Dudodyn
Llyn Peris
Afon Gafr
Y Garn
Tryfan
Cwm Clyd
Llyn Idwal
Llugwy
Llyn Bychan
Reservoir
Llyn Goddi duon
Capel Curig
10
Nant Peris
Llyn-y-Cwn
Cefn-y-Capel
Pinnacle Café
A5
Afon Las
Glyder Fawr
Glyder Fach
Snowdon Mountain Railway
Pass of Llanberis
A4086
Llyn Cwm ffynnon
A4086
Llynnau mymbyr
Pont Cyfyng
11
Afon Nantygwryd
Mynydd Cribe
Crib y Ddysgl
Crib Goch
Pen-y-Gwryd Hotel
Llyn Llydaw
Carnedd Moel Siabod
Llyn-y-Foel
Glaslyn
Cwm Dyli
A498
Llyaau Diwaunedd
Pont-y-pant
SNOWDON
Falls
Lechog
Y Lliwedd
Gallt-y-Wenallt
Craig Du
Dolwyddelan
Cwm Caregog
Cwm-y-Llan
Llyn Gwynant
Pentre-bont
Blaenau Dolwyddelan
Y Geuallt
Yr Aran
Graig Wen
Glanaber
Cwm Edno
Yr Arddu
Bethania
Bryn-y-dinas
Plas Gwynant
Moel Meirch
Ro Wen
A498
Llyn Edno
Llyn Dinas
Afon Llyn
Ysgafell Wen
A470
Moel llechwedd Hafod
12
Sygun Copper Mine
Moel Penamnen
Llynau-y-Cwn
Glandyr Café
Beddgelert
Llynau yr Adar
C
Llynnau Cerrig-y-my-llt
Llyn Conglog
Tal-y-waenydd
Scale
I Mile
I Km
Llyn Cwmorthin
Rhiwbryfdir
Blaenau Ffestiniog

7 TL at first junction (10.5km/6.5 miles). Pass Dinas Farm campsite.

8 SO at junction then immediately TL at TJ (by telephone).

9 TR at TJ, SP A5/Betws-y-coed (14km/ 8.5 miles). Continue on road as it climbs to Llyn Ogwen and then gradually descends to Capel Curig.

10 TR at TJ onto A4086, SP Caernarfon. ***29km (18 miles)***

11 SO at junction by Pen-y-Gwryd Hotel onto A498, SP Beddgelert/Porthmadog. Continue into Beddgelert, passing Sygun Copper Mine. ***36km (22.5 miles)***

12 SO at junction by bridge in Beddgelert onto A4085 (48km/30 miles), SP Caernarfon. Climb to Rhyd-Ddu.

13 TL at TJ onto B4418, SP Nantlle/ Penygroes (54km/33.5 miles). After initial climb the road descends quickly through Drws-y-Coed to Nantlle. Continue to Talysarn and cross concrete bridge.

14 TL at TJ, SP Penygroes (63.5km/ 39.5 miles). Pass leisure centre on RHS.

15 TL into Victoria Road.

16 SO at XR, SP Lôn Eifion Cycleway. DO NOT join cycleway but follow road over bridge.

17 SO at junction. ***66.5km (41.5 miles)***

18 TR at TJ onto A499, SP Caernarfon. Continue and pass Glynllifon Park.

19 TL at SECOND junction after Glynllifon Park, SP Llandwrog (70.5km/44 miles). Continue into Llandwrog.

20 TR at junction (opposite Hart Hotel, after church in Llandwrog). Follow road through Saron (75.5km/47 miles). Continue over bridge and SO at junction (DO NOT follow SP Beach). Continue through Llanfaglan. Pass Hospital on RHS, descend steeply and then immediately:

21 TL before main road into Coed Helen Road (78.5km/49 miles). Cycle uphill and cross river into Caernarfon via footbridge. Keep L along seafront to Victoria Dock and join Lôn Las Menai Cycleway by Safeway carpark.

22 Take second exit at roundabout, SP Bangor–Cyclists (84.5km/52.5 miles). Continue through Port Dinorwig.

23 TL at roundabout, SP Holyhead/Conwy/ A487, for climb.

24 TR at roundabout (under expressway), SP Bangor/Conwy. ***90.5km (56 miles)***

25 SO at roundabout, SP Bangor.

26 TL at roundabout by Antelope Hotel, SP Menai Bridge. Cross bridge and SO at roundabout to return to car park and the end of the route. ***95km (59 miles)***

To return to Bangor station, SO at roundabout and TR into station at traffic lights.

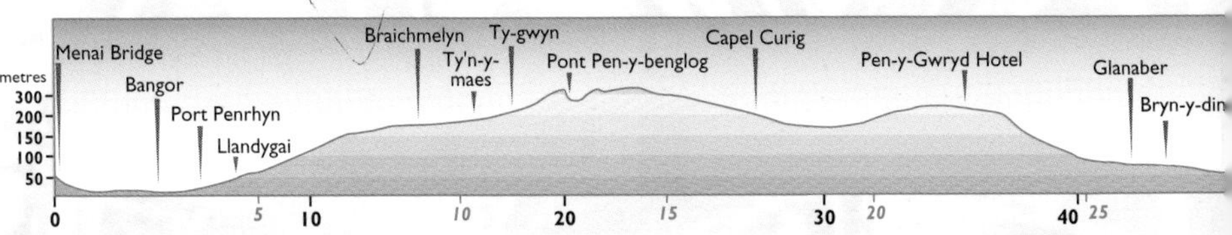

Places of interest along the route

A Menai Suspension Bridge

Built by Thomas Telford between 1819 and 1826 and 30.5m (100 feet) high. This was the first permanent crossing of the Menai Strait. Before construction of the bridge, the crossing had to be made by ferry: animals, on their way to and from market, had to swim. Britannia Bridge is a combined rail and road bridge and was built by Robert Stephenson between 1846 and 1850.

B Bangor

There has been a settlement here for hundreds of years. In the 6th century St Deiniol founded a monastery and the name Bangor is said to come from the Welsh word Bangori, used to describe the wattle fence which must have surrounded his community's buildings. **Bangor Cathedral** dates from the 13th century and was restored in 1866. Close by is a biblical garden, containing plants associated with the Bible. **Penrhyn Castle** dates from the 19th century and is owned by the National Trust. The grounds offer stunning views of Snowdonia and the Menai Strait. Tearoom. Open March to October, Wednesday–Monday; castle 1200–1700; grounds 1100–1700. Charge. Telephone (01248) 353084. There is much else to see in Bangor. Contact the town's Tourist Information centre for more information on (01248) 352786.

C Beddgelert

At the heart of Snowdonia National Park, the village is surrounded by mountains. Beddgelert was a great religious centre and also a port, access by boat made possible by the River Glaslyn until the Porthmadog embankment was constructed during the 19th century. Just outside the village is **Sygun Copper Mine** where visitors can explore the old mine workings and traces of precious metals. Also visitor centre and tearoom. Open Easter to September, daily 1000–1700; October to March telephone to confirm. Charge. Telephone (01766) 510101.

D Caernarfon

The walled town of Caernarfon is situated overlooking the Menai Strait and is dominated by its castle. There is much to see in and around the town. See route 5 for further details.

Food and drink

Plenty of choice in Bangor and Caernarfon. Refreshments are also available at Penrhyn Castle and Sygun Copper Mine.

Pinnacle Café, Capel Curig
Teas, coffees and snacks available.

Glandyr Café, Beddgelert
On the RHS over the bridge in Bedgelert.

Cwellyn Arms, Rhyd Ddu
Good bar food available here.

Anglesey Arms, Menai Bridge
By the suspension bridge. Bar meals available.

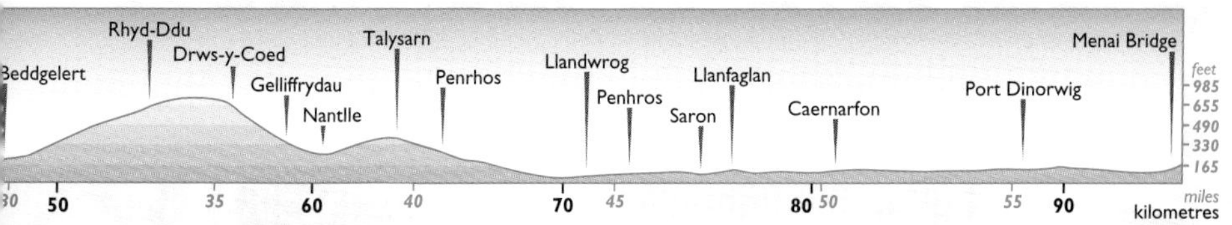

Route **25**

SNOWDONIA – A GRANDE RANDONNÉE

Route information

Distance 115.5km (72 miles)

Grade Strenuous

Terrain Flat ground at sea level, two long climbs and a long steady descent into the Conwy valley at Betws-y-coed. Often the hills are bare and rocky, but in several places they are well wooded with many streams. Buzzards and red kites are likely to be seen anywhere on the route.

Time to allow 1–2 days.

Getting there by car Betws-y-coed is on the A5 and can also be reached via the A55 and A470. There are two public car parks opposite the railway station in Betws-y-coed, one free and the other pay and display.

Getting there by train Trains bound for Blaenau Ffestiniog call at Betws-y-coed. Telephone (0345) 484950 for travel information.

This route covers the centre of Snowdonia National Park, mostly via main roads since there are not many other roads of any sort that lend themselves to a circuit of the central massif of the park. However, the roads are generally quiet, except at weekends during the height of the holiday season. From Betws-y-coed the route heads south west, to Blaenau Ffestiniog and Aberglaslyn. On to Tremadog, where the route picks up the Lôn Las Eifion long distance cycleway towards Caernarfon, part of the National Cycle Route. The route now turns east returning to Betws-y-coed via Llanberis. Since Porthmadog and Caernarfon are both busy places, particularly in the holiday season, the route bypasses them but the route directions indicate where to make diversions if you wish to visit these places, and it would be a shame not to do so. There are so many interesting places to see en route that you might want to tackle it over a couple of days. The local Tourist Information Centres (see page 13) can provide general information and an advance booking service for all types of accommodation.

Route description

Exit car park and head towards the town (station on LHS).

1 TL at TJ onto A5, no SP. Cross Waterloo Bridge.

2 Immediately follow A5 round to R and TR onto A470, SP Dolgellau/ Blaenau Ffestiniog. This is the start of a long climb up the Lledr valley. Continue through Dolwyddelan (9.5km/ 6 miles) with castle ruins on RHS outside village. Arrive summit (15.5km/ 9.5 miles) for steep, twisting descent. Continue, passing Llechwedd Slate Caverns on LHS.

3 To visit Blaenau Ffestiniog, TL at roundabout. After visit, retrace to roundabout and TL onto A496.

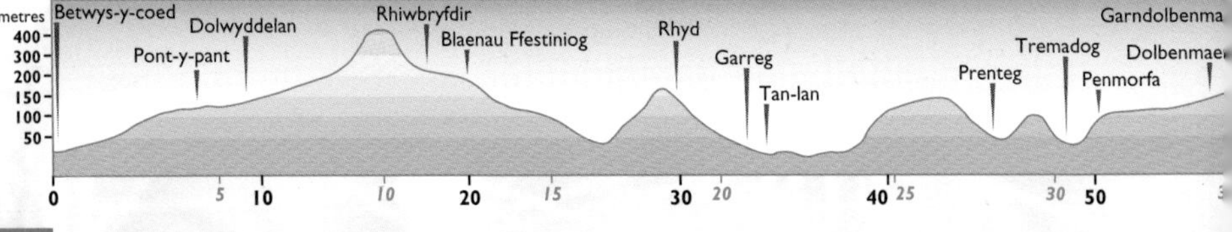

Otherwise, to continue route, TR at roundabout onto A496, SP Porthmadog/Dolgellau/Bala.

4 TR WITH CARE (on L bend with poor visibility) onto unclassified road, SP Workshops.

5 TL by SP No Through Road/Maentwrog/ train symbol. ***20km (12.5 miles)***

6 To visit Ffestiniog Power Station take sharp TR at junction with A496 onto minor road.

Otherwise, to continue route, TR at TJ onto A496, SP Maentwrog, for a long and sometimes steep, descent. Continue until approach to main road – the next turn is easy to miss.

7 Immediately before TJ with main road, TR into unclassified road (by SP width restriction). The surface of this minor road is reasonable but beware loose gravel, sheep and farm dogs. ***24km (15 miles)***

8 TR at TJ onto A487, no SP.

9 TR onto B4410, SP Rhyd (by Oakeley Arms Hotel). Pass under railway bridge (29km/18 miles) and continue on this road.

10 TR at staggered XR onto A4085, SP Beddgelert. ***33.5km (21 miles)***

11 TL at TJ onto A498, SP Porthmadog. To visit Porthmadog/Portmeirion TL in Tremadog. Otherwise, to continue route, follow A487, SP Caernarfon.

12 TR into Hen Lon (road name), no SP. ***50km (31 miles)***

13 TR at TJ and follow SP Cycleway.

14 Keep L and follow SP Cycleway.

15 TR at TJ onto A487, no SP.

16 TR, SP Garndolbenmaen. ***56km (35 miles)***

17 SO uphill (by new style telephone box where main road turns sharply L).

18 TL at TJ, no SP. ***60km (37.5 miles)***

19 SO WITH CARE over busy road, through gates to Derwyn Fawr (private road) for 50m. TR through small wooden gate onto Lôn Las Eifion cycleway, no SP. Continue towards Caernarfon.

20 The cycleway is interrupted here (74km/46 miles) by the A499 and the route now bypasses Caernarfon. To visit Caernarfon cross A499 WITH CARE to pick up cycleway on other side and follow it into Caernarfon. After visit, follow A4086, SP Llanberis, and rejoin route at direction 24, where TL.

Otherwise, to continue route, TR onto A499

21 SO at roundabout, SP Caernarfon.

22 TR, SP Llanberis.

23 SO at roundabout, SP Llanberis. ***79.5km (49.5 miles)***

24 TR at TJ, SP Llanberis. Continue and keep right to go through Llanberis (90km/ 56 miles). Continue through Nant Peris for long climb to summit at Pen-y-Pass. Views of Crib Goch and Snowdon on RHS, Glyder Mountains on LHS. The road narrows and traffic is slow moving, so take extra care. Arrive summit (99km/61.5 miles). There is a café on RHS by car park. Continue for fast descent.

25 TL at TJ, SP Capel Curig.

26 TR at TJ, SP Betws-y-coed.

27 Pass Swallow Falls on LHS, only impressive after a lot of rain. ***113km (70 miles)***

28 TL to return to Betws-y-coed station and the end of the ride. ***115.5km (72 miles)***

yncir
Graianog
Penygroes
Dolydd
Bontnewydd
Pont-rug
Cwm-y-glo
Llanrug
Llanberis
Nant Peris
Pen-y-Gwryd Hotel
Capel Curig
Glyn
Betwys-y-coed
feet 1310 985 655 490 330 165
60 40 70 45 80 50 55 90 60 100 65 110 70
miles
kilometres

B4419
N
Menai Strait
Dismantled railway
A487
B4366
Afon Seiont
Saron
Llanddeiniolen
Bethel
Rhiwlas
Douglas Hill
Penrhyn Slate Quarries
Llyn-y-Mynydd
Waen
Penisar Waun
Rhiwen
Waterloo Port
Afon Cadnant
24
A4086
B4547
Deiniolen
Carnedd-y-Filiast
Plas Penrhyn
E
Caernarfon
Pont-rug
Llanrug
Brynrefail
Clwt-y-bont
Maes Caradoc
Res.
Cwm-y-glo
Llanberis Lake Railway
Fachwen
Gallt-y-foel
Marchlyn Mawr Res.
Penrhos
23
Tyddyn hwys-gynt
Ceunant
Llyn Padarn
Elidyr Fach
Foel Goch
Hen-dy
Ysgulor Isaf
Dinorwig
Fuches-las
Llanberis
Hafotty
Afon Dudodyn
Tyddyn Eleu
Roman Road
A4085
Groeslon
Cefn Du
Llanfaglan
F
Llyn Peris
Afon Gafr
Bontnewydd
Afon Gwynfai
22
Waunfawr
Dinas
Nant-y-Bettws
Nant Peris
Saron
Afon Las
Wernlas
Afon Arddu
Snowdon Mountain Railway
Pass of
Llanwnda
21
Betws Garmon
Cwm Dwythwch
20
Rhostryfan
Moel Smytho
A4086
Bethesda
Dolydd
Rhosgadfan
Salem
Foel Goch
Moel Tryfan
Llandwrog
Afon Llifon
Llyn Cwellyn
Crib Goch
Glynllifon Park
Groeslon
Craig Cwm Bychan
Crib y Ddysgl
Llyn y Ffynnonau
Carmel
Glaslyn
Glynllifon
Uwchlawr-rhos
Mynydd Mawr
Llyn Coch
Mynydd Cilgwyn
Fron
Llyn Nadroedd
SNOWDON
Craig y Bera
Llyn Dywarchen
Cilgwyn
Gelliffrydau
Lechog
Penygroes
Talysarn
Nantlle
Drws-y-Coed
Rhyd-Ddu
Craig Du
Cwm Caregog
Eithinog
B4418
Cwm-y-Llan
Llyn Nantlle Uchaf
Y Garn
Y Geuallt
Lleuer-fach
Trum-y-Ddysgl
Ffridd Uchaf
Yr Aran
Llanllyfni
Pitts Head
Craig Wen
Afon Crychddw
Craig Cwm Silyn
Bethania
Llwyn-bedw
Nebo
Afon Ddu
Llynau Cwm Silyn
BEDDGELERT
Bryn-y-dinas
Llyn Llewelyn
Nasareth
Garnedd-goch
Llynau Cwmdulyn
Llyn Dinas
raianog
FOREST
A498
A487
Cwm Trwsg
Braich-y-dinas
Nant Gwynant
Moel Lefn
Mynydd Craig goch
Cwm Ciprwt
Beddgelert
Tyddyn-mawr
Cwm Cloch
Moel y Dyniewyd
Bwlch Meillionen
Nantmor
Pant-glas
Brithdir
Pont Aberglaslyn
Upper Clynnog
Craig Lwyd
Cwm Llefrith
Moel Hebog
Afon Goch
11
Bwlch Derwin
Bwlch-derwydd
Nantmor
18
A4085
19
Ceunant Ddo
Llyn Oerddwr
Llanfihangel-y-Pennant
Mynydd Cennin
Cennin
Craig-y-Garn
Llyn Cwmystradllyn
Bryncir
Moel Ddu
A498
Hendre Cenin
Tyddyndu
17
Garndolbenmaen
Braich-y-big
Tyddyn-mawr
16
Brynkir
Tan-lan
Llecheiddior
Dolbenmaen
Glan Dwyfach
15
Golan
14
Afon Cwmystradllyn
Llyn Du
Afon Glaslyn
Mynydd Gorllwyn
10
Ford
A487
Traeth Mawr
Ystum Cegid
Afon Ddu
B4410
Garreg
13
12
Prenteg
Afon Dwyfach
Rhoslan
Allt Wen
A498
Morfa Gwyllt
A4085
Ymwlch fawr
Penmorfa
Ty-mawr
Pentrefelin
Wern
A498
Tremadog
Afon Dwyfor
Gell
Porthmadog
Y Garth
B4411
A497
Pen-amser
D
A487
Llanystumdwy
Criccieth
To Portmeirion
Minffordd

Ogwen Bank
Yr Elan
Gledr Ffordd
Llyn Eigiau Reservoir
Ddu
Carnedd Llywelyn
Pen-bryn-brwynog
Careg-wen
Craig yr Ysfa
Ty'n-y-maes
Nant Fuch
Pen-y-Waen Wen
Trefriw
Llanddoged
Ysgolion Duon
Ty-gwyn
Fynnon Llugwy Reservoir
Pen Helig
Llyn Cowlyd Reservoir
Cefn Cyfarwydd
Nant Ffranco
Ffynnon Laer
Pen Llithrig-y-wrach
Creigiau Gleision
Llyn Crafnant
Llanrwst
Llyn Geirionydd
Llyn Ogwen
A5
Melin-y-coed
Cwm Clyd
Tryfan
Llyn Idwal
Llyn Bychan
Llyn Bedgynydd
Llyn-y-Parc
Reservoir
Llyn Goddion-duon
Llugwy
Llyn-y-Cwn
26
Capel Curig
Cefn-y-Capel
Glyder Fawr
Glyder Fach
Glyn
Swallow Falls
B5106
River Conwy
A470
A4086
Dol-gam
27
Pont Cyfyng
Llynnau mymbyr
Llyn Cwm ffynnon
Llanberis
Nantygwryd
28
1
Betws-y-coed
A
25
Pen-y-Gwryd Hotel
Mynydd Cribau
2
Llyn Llydaw
Carnedd Moel Siabod
Llyn-y-Foel
Llyn Reservoir
Cwm Dyli
A498
Llydau Diwaunedd
Ystumiau
Pont-y-pant
Valley
Lledr
Gallt-y-Wenallt
Falls
Conwy Falls
Pandy Mill and Falls
Tan-y-clogwyn
Messhill
Dolwyddelan
Castle (ruins)
Llyn Gwynant
Diwaunedd
Gwibernant
Iwerddon
Machno
B4406
Blaenau Dolwyddelan
Pentre-bont
Bwlch-y-groes
Gwydyr Forest
Cwm Edno
Glanaber
Plas Gwynant
Penmachno
Moel Meirch
Y Ro-Lwyd
Yr Arddu
Ro Wen
Llyn Edno
Afon Llyn
Ysgafell Wen
Moel llechwedd Hafod
Oernant
Llynau-y-Cwn
Moel Penamnen
Cwn Penmachno
Llynau yr Adar
Carrog
Llynnau Cerrig-y-my-llt
Tal-y-waenydd
Llyn Newydd
Glanaber Terrace
Llyn Conglog
Llechwedd Slate Caverns
Llyn Bowydd
Pen y bedw
Rhiwbryfdir
Moel Manchyria
Llyn Cwmorthin
5
3
Llyn Conwy
Hafnant
Blaenau Ffestiniog
B
Cwm Croesor
Ffestiniog Power Station Visitor Centre
4
C
6
Bethania
Craig Goch
Bryn Mawr
Swlan Reservoir
Tanygrisiau Reservoir
Scale
1 Mile
1 Km
Moelwyn Bach
Ffestiniog Railway
A470
Teigl
B4407
Migneint
Llyn Morwynion
Gam
Rhyd
7
8
Llyn Dywarchen
B4391
Ffestiniog
Nant y Groes
A496
B4391
Cwm-Cynfal
B4410
Bont Newydd
Carnedd Lago
Tai-luirion
Maentwrog
A487
9
Gellilydan
Graig Wen
Llyngraig-wen
Taihirion
A496
Craig Gyfynys
Llyn Conglog-mawr
Moel y-Groesau
A4212

Places of interest along the route

A Betws-y-coed

A small, busy town at the confluence of the Rivers Llugwy, Lledr and Conwy. Waterloo Bridge at the southern end of the town was designed and built by the famous civil engineer, Thomas Telford, and was the only such structure he made with ornate embellishments. See route 21 for more information.

B Blaenau Ffestiniog

The mountain terminus of the Ffestiniog Mountain Railway which runs from Porthmadog. The town is also home to the **Llechwedd Slate Caverns**, spectacular underground caverns which can be explored via two tours. For further information see route 6.

C Ffestiniog Power Station Visitor Centre, near Blaenau Ffestiniog

This was the UK's first pumped storage electricity generating station and is well worth a visit. See route 6 for more details.

D Porthmadog and Portmeiron

Although the route does not pass through Porthmadog, a short diversion will take you to this popular holiday destination. See route 6 for more information. The mock Italianate village of Portmeirion, made famous by the cult television series *The Prisoner*, is only 3km (2 miles) from Porthmadog. Again, see route 6 for more information.

E Caernarfon

The walled town of Caernarfon is situated overlooking the Menai Strait and is dominated by the castle. There is much to see in and around the town. See route 5 for further details.

Snowdon Mountain Railway

Food and drink

Plenty of choice in all the towns passed through en route and refreshments are available at many of the places of interest.

F Llanberis

As well as the starting point of the most straight forward walking route up the mountain, Llanberis is also home to the **Snowdon Mountain Railway**, the country's only public rack and pinion railway, which opened in 1896. The train runs right up to the summit of Snowdon (1085m/3560 feet), affording spectacular views on a clear day. The trains are usually full to capacity during fine weather so you should arrive early if you wish to take the train to the summit. Café at the station and the summit. Open March–October, daily; trains run between 0900 and 1700 but times are subject to change. Charge. Telephone (01286) 870223. **Padarn Park** at Llanberis offers another railway journey – the Llanberis Lake Railway will take you along the shore of Padarn Lake on narrow gauge steam trains. The park also contains picnic sites, a nature trail, and old slate quarry, historic hospital, slate museum, water wheel and café. Open March to October, Monday–Thursday; also open Friday–Sunday during summer. Small charge. Telephone (01286) 870549. **Electric Mountain** offers visitors a tour around the fastest man-made electricity generator in Europe, set inside the largest man-made cavern in Europe. As well as tours, there is a visitor centre and coffee shop on site. Open Easter to Christmas, daily; telephone to confirm opening hours. Charge for tours only. Telephone (01286) 870636.

THE CTC

The CTC is Britain's largest national cycling organisation. Founded in 1878, the CTC has over 65,000 members and affiliates throughout the UK, and around 230 local groups. The CTC provides essential services for all leisure cyclists, whether riding on- or off-road, and works to promote cycling and protect cyclists' interests.

Free technical and touring advice

CTC membership makes day-to-day cycling easier. A resident expert cycling engineer answers technical queries about cycle buying, maintenance and equipment. And if you get ambitious about your cycling, the CTC's Touring Department has reams of information about cycling anywhere from Avon to Zimbabwe. Then, when it comes to getting kitted out, the CTC's mail order shop sells a wide variety of clothing and accessories in addition to books, maps and guidebooks, including other titles from HarperCollins Publishers.

CTC Helpdesk – telephone (01483) 417217

CTC members also receive *Cycle Touring and Campaigning* magazine free six times a year. *CT&C* takes pride in its journalistic independence. With reports on cycle trips all over the globe, forensic tests on bikes and equipment, and the most vigorous and effective pro-bike campaigning stance anywhere, *CT&C* is required reading for any cyclist.

CTC membership costs from £15 p.a.

It is not just members who benefit. The CTC works on behalf of all Britain's 22 million cycle owners. Its effective campaigning at national level helped to create the Government's National Cycling Strategy. It is lobbying for lower speed limits on country lanes; campaigning so that you can carry bikes on trains; working with Local Authorities to make towns more cycle-friendly, to ensure that roads are designed to meet cyclists' needs and kept well maintained; making sure that bridleways are kept open; and negotiating cyclists' access to canal towpaths.

Whatever kind of cyclist you are – mountain biker, Sunday potterer, bicycle commuter, or out for the day with your family – cycling is easier and safer with the CTC's knowledge and services in your saddlebag. The CTC is the essential accessory for every cyclist!

For further information contact:
CTC
69 Meadrow
Godalming
Surrey
GU7 3HS

Telephone (01483) 417217
Fax (01483) 426994
e-mail: cycling@ctc.org.uk
Website: http://www.ctc.org.uk